How
Psychic
are You?

hamlyn

How
Psychic
are You?

UNDERSTAND AND DEVELOP
YOUR NATURAL ABILITY

Paul Roland

This book is affectionately dedicated to my 'circle' of intuitive friends Sylvia Gainsford, Tamara Mount, Jill Nash, Karin Page and Betty Shine.

A Pyramid Paperback

First published in Great Britain in 2006 by Hamlyn, a division of Octopus Publishing Group Ltd, 2–4 Heron Quays, London E14 4JP

Copyright © Octopus Publishing Group Limited 2006

Distributed in the United States and Canada by Sterling Publishing Co., Inc., 387 Park Avenue South, New York, NY 10016-8810

The right of Paul Roland to be identified as the author of this work has been asserted by him in accordance with the Copyright, Designs and Patents Act, 1988.

This material was previously published as *How Psychic are You?*

ISBN-13: 978-0-600-61471-5
ISBN-10: 0-600-61471-9

A CIP catalogue record for this book is available from the British Library

Printed and bound in China

10 9 8 7 6 5 4 3 2 1

PUBLISHER'S NOTE
The exercises in this book are intended for relaxation and increasing self-awareness. However, if you have recently experienced mental or emotional problems or are taking medication you should seek professional medical advice before practising these exercises on your own. The author and publisher accept no responsibility for any harm caused by or to anyone as a result of the misuse of these exercises.

For practical purposes it is recommended that you record the scripts of the various exercises onto cassette so that you do not have to continually refer to the text. For the more simple visualizations you might find that a background of suitably inspiring music or natural sound effects can create a relaxing atmosphere.

Contents

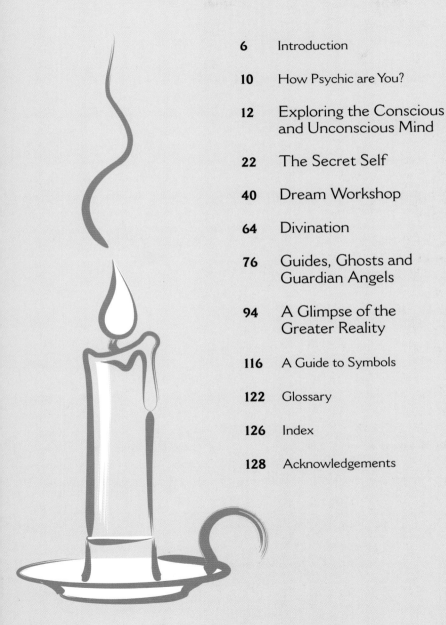

6   Introduction

10   How Psychic are You?

12   Exploring the Conscious and Unconscious Mind

22   The Secret Self

40   Dream Workshop

64   Divination

76   Guides, Ghosts and Guardian Angels

94   A Glimpse of the Greater Reality

116   A Guide to Symbols

122   Glossary

126   Index

128   Acknowledgements

Introduction

What does 'psychic' actually mean?

The term psychic is derived from the Greek word 'psukhe', meaning soul, and can be applied to either a person who claims to have developed a 'sixth sense', or an ability which appears to be outside the possibilities determined by natural laws. This would include all forms of extrasensory perception (ESP), telepathy, the ability to foretell future events, psychometry (the capacity to derive impressions of people and places from objects) and the extension of awareness to another location commonly known as remote viewing. For that reason such talents are often described as supernatural and are generally considered to be beyond the limits of 'normal' human experience. However, practising psychics, or 'sensitives' as many prefer to be called, consider that the supernatural is merely an extension of the natural world and that all psychic experiences conform to universal rather than physical laws. Such experiences are often confused with paranormal phenomena which is a broad, catch-all category for any incident or experience which defies a rational explanation.

What are psychic powers?

Those who claim to possess psychic ability consider it to be an innate sixth sense that we all possess, but which few of us have considered developing because Western culture has conditioned us to refute anything which cannot be measured by rigorous scientific analysis. Psychics do not consider their abilities super-human but simply an acute sensitivity to the subtle energies surrounding all living things and a heightened awareness of a greater reality which exists beyond our physical world. In the case of remote viewing or out-of-body experiences (OBEs) this could involve the extension of one's awareness to another location.

Is there any proof?

There have been many stringent scientific experiments since the 1960s, which have provided irrefutable proof of the existence of psychic ability in certain individuals, some of which will be described in the appropriate sections of this book. One of the most significant was that published in 1994 by the prestigious American journal *Psychological Bulletin*, which reported an impressive 34 per cent success rate during an extensive experiment into ESP over the course of several years.

In addition I will be drawing upon the anecdotal evidence of several psychics with whom I have worked over the years and that of students who have attended my psychic development courses. I will also add my own personal experiences where relevant. But the real proof will come as you use the exercises described at key points throughout this book to test, identify and measure the level of your own developing psychic sensitivity.

Is everyone psychic?

Clearly few of us possess the abilities demonstrated by 'celebrity psychics' such as Uri Geller, Ingo Swann, James Van Praagh, John Edward or Betty Shine, but who has not experienced déjà vu, or has sensed that a friend or family member will telephone moments before they call? Unfortunately, we tend to dismiss such events as a product of our imagination, or as mere coincidence, because we have been conditioned from childhood to be rational and to believe that imagination, dreams and intuition have no value and can be of no practical use. The most common forms of psychic phenomena, such as ESP and OBEs, often occur involuntarily at times of extreme stress or during an illness when the bond between mind and body are disturbed. They are therefore frequently dismissed as merely the product of an unsettled mind.

A 1984 survey for *Time-Life* magazine in the USA revealed that 75 per cent of all Americans claimed to have had some form of psychic experience. Interestingly, women were more likely to have had personal experience of psychic phenomena than men, which suggests that women tend to trust their intuition and feelings more than men whose rational mentality might be filtering out the more subtle impressions. Since the late 1980s the proportion of those claiming psychic experience has increased, no doubt because of the emergence of the New Age movement which has made such experiences more socially acceptable. From similar surveys conducted since the 1960s and the wealth of anecdotal evidence collected by SPR (the Society for Psychical Research) and ASSAP (the Association for the Scientific Study of Anomalous Phenomena), organizations thriving in the UK and USA, it would appear that psychic experience is more common than we might imagine.

How do I develop my powers?

The simple exercises in this book will help you to identify, develop and employ your psychic abilities and reveal latent talents of which you are not currently aware. But you are going to have to be prepared to see the world from an entirely new perspective.

By developing your psychic powers you are making a significant step towards self-awareness and the fulfilment of your true potential. The more we learn about ourselves the closer we can come to realizing our true nature – which is immortal and divine. On a practical level psychic insight brings greater self-confidence and freedom from fear, which is the most significant handicap to progress and self-realization that we impose upon ourselves.

Is there any danger?

I have been practising meditation and many forms of spiritual self-development for more than 30 years and I have never had an unpleasant experience or encountered anything to fear. The only thing to be wary of is the negative energy of other people (which you can easily protect yourself from) and your own fears which can be overcome. The more you learn about yourself and your true nature, the more confident and self-assured you will become.

Will I be dabbling with the occult?

If you approach psychic work as a form of self-development and avoid dabbling with Ouija boards and invoking spirits there is nothing to fear. If, however, you feel uncomfortable for any reason during one of the exercises you can simply count down slowly from ten to one and open your eyes, or practise the grounding exercise on page 24. Remember that at all times you are in control. Moreover, it is said that 'like attracts like', which means that if your intentions are good and your search for insight is sincere you will receive help, guidance and protection at all times.

Real or just my imagination?

As you develop your psychic awareness the quality of your experiences will intensify, confirming what you previously only sensed or suspected. During 'readings' the impressions that you receive from family members, friends or clients will become stronger and the images will be more vivid. You will 'see' with a new clarity in much the same way as a short-sighted person sees the world in a new way after being fitted with glasses.

Initially you will need to test yourself, analyse the results and measure your progress with the exercises, but within six months you should be able to distinguish between genuine psychic experiences and the products of your imagination. Psychic impressions are quite distinct from the products of the imagination. They arise spontaneously and cannot be manipulated or distorted at will. They appear to have a life of their own and you may 'see' scenes or flashes from a past life, or glimpses of the future, as if you were watching a film. Psychic experiences seem more 'real' than those of everyday existence as our sixth sense is more acute than our five physical senses.

This book aims to allay any fears that you might have of the unknown and will dispel some of the popular misconceptions and take the sensationalism out of the subject of psychic ability. Using safe and simple exercises it will show how you can awaken your dormant psychic talents to become more self-aware, confident and in control of your own life. Each chapter will describe the practical applications of specific abilities and will include a number of simple exercises to encourage you to recognize, measure and develop your latent powers.

What psychic abilities can I acquire?

Once you learn to trust your intuition you should be able to practise psychometry, psychic healing, reading the aura (the human energy field) to determine an individual's health and state of mind, and explore the inner world of the Unconscious for insight, guidance and greater self-awareness. Psychic abilities are similar to other talents in that we each have a natural aptitude in a specific area – but you won't know where your strengths lie until you have worked through all the exercises in this book. No one talent is more significant than any other. But the degree to which that talent is developed depends on the individual. Obviously, someone with real insight and a genuine empathy for their clients is going to be of considerably more value than a part-time 'professional' manning a so-called psychic phone-line.

How Psychic are You?

20 key questions to test your PSI rating

1   Have you ever had an out-of-body experience?

2   Do you sometimes 'know' in advance that a friend or family member is going to ring you or visit unexpectedly?

3   Have you ever found yourself in a situation that seems strangely familiar and yet you are sure that you haven't experienced it before?

4   Have you ever been overwhelmed by an unaccountable negative feeling towards a stranger or someone you have just met?

5   Have you ever sensed that someone has had the ability to calm and comfort you just by being near you?

6   Can you ease physical pain simply by laying your hand on the affected part of your own or another person's body?

7   Have you ever been disturbed by a negative atmosphere at a particular place which you later learnt was the location of a violent incident or the scene of suffering?

8   Can you sense the serenity in a sacred place such as a church or in a room where people practise meditation?

9   Have you ever seen a ghost or sensed an unseen presence?

10 Have you ever smelt the distinctive fragrance of a loved one who is deceased?

11 Are you sensitive to the energy of minerals and plants? Can you feel a tingling sensation when handling a crystal?

12 Have you ever sensed a presence when there was no one near you or felt what could be described as cobwebs touching your skin?

13 Have you ever had a vision or knowledge of a future event that you have later been able to verify?

14 Can you see a vivid blue outline or any other colour(s) around people with whom you have an affinity?

15 Do you ever have dreams that seem more real than your everyday experience?

16 Have you ever dreamt about a loved one who has died and woken with a sense that it was not a dream at all, but that it might have been a real encounter?

17 Have you ever been apart from someone who is close to you and instinctively known what they were doing and later discovered that you were right?

18 Have you ever seen a single unblinking eye staring back at you when you close your eyes and are relaxed?

19 When someone tells you of their plans do you ever have a strong feeling how it will turn out? And have you been proved right?

20 Do you have a strong affinity to a particular period in history and a nagging suspicion that a particular place and time were significant for you in a past life?

Your answers

If you answered **'yes'** to three or more of the questions then you clearly have psychic ability that can be developed. All you need is to become conscious of the subtle influences at work in yourself and the world around you and learn to activate your innate abilities at will.

If you answered **'no'** to all of the questions it would appear that you're denying this aspect of yourself, either because you are anxious what might happen if you open up to unseen influences, or because you have been conditioned to believe that psychic phenomena is irrational, has something to do with the occult and is therefore dangerous.

In either case, the exercises and personal experiences described in the following pages should convince you that there is nothing unnatural in awakening your True Nature or heightening your awareness of the worlds beyond the physical senses. Certainly, there is nothing to fear 'out there' or within. In fact, our health, happiness and personal growth depend upon self-exploration.

Exploring the Conscious and Unconscious Mind

The clinical definition of the unconscious mind is that part of our mind where the instincts, impulses, images, ideas, memories and deepest fears that are not available for direct examination reside. It is distinct from the subconscious, which is that part of the mind that is on the periphery of our awareness and contains material which we can become conscious of simply by directing our attention to it. In this section you will find methods for expanding consciousness to enable you to connect with your Higher Self for greater insight and heightening psychic awareness.

Exercise 1: Expanding Consciousness
Exercise 2: Entering the Light
Exercise 3: The Garden
Exercise 4: The Inner Journey
Exercise 5: Exploring the Path of the Psyche

What is the Unconscious?

A Verbal Warning

Several times during the London Blitz the British Prime Minister Winston Churchill was saved by an inner voice that warned him of danger. On one occasion Churchill heard a voice say 'stop!' as he was about to climb into the car on the left side which was being held open for him by his driver. So he walked around to the other side, leaving his driver surprised and confused. During their journey a bomb exploded next to the car, piercing the rear left side with shrapnel. Churchill would have been killed had he been sitting in his usual seat. On another occasion he left a dinner party to warn his kitchen staff to go down to the shelter. A few minutes later a bomb scored a direct hit on the kitchen. Churchill didn't say whether he believed the voice was his Unconscious or his Guardian Angel; he was just grateful to have heard it in time.

Psychics and those with a more spiritual world view make a slight but significant distinction between the subconscious and the unconscious minds. They believe that the subconscious mind contains the impulses, instincts, images, ideas, memories and fears that reside just below the surface of our everyday waking awareness, while the Unconscious is the immortal aspect of our personality, our essence or Higher Self, which is the source of all our ideas, intuition and inspiration.

Tapping into the Unconscious

The key to psychic awareness is establishing a strong connection with the unconscious mind, which has chosen to use a body as a vehicle for learning through experience, in one life after another. Consciousness is not to be confused with the activities of the brain, which is a purely physical organ acting as a receiver of sensory input – in a similar way to that in which a radio translates signals into sound. Consciousness is formless mental energy and is therefore capable of expanding beyond the limits of the physical form to link up with what is sometimes called the Universal Consciousness, or Collective Consciousness. The latter is a term created by Carl Jung, the father of modern psychoanalysis, who defined the Collective Unconscious as the primal level of the psyche where the universal archetypal symbols of our more significant dreams have their existence. This matrix

Exercise 1: Expanding Consciousness

This exercise provides the first step towards projecting consciousness to another location (as in remote viewing) by requiring you to become aware that your mind is a formless matrix of energy and is not confined to the brain.

◆ Sit in a straight-backed chair with your feet flat on the floor and slightly apart. You can rest your hands on your knees or in your lap with your fingers intertwined and the palms facing upward.

◆ Take a slow, deep breath and exhale until the last particle of stale air has been expelled from your lungs. Now establish a regular, even rhythm of breathing, exhaling and inhaling for a count of four and pausing between breaths for a count of two.

◆ Now let your mind go blank. Don't think of anything. Just concentrate on breath control. When thoughts occur observe them with detachment and let them go. Don't attach any significance to them.

◆ Bring your mind gently back to your breath. If you have difficulties focusing on emptiness you can visualize a blank white wall or a blackboard, but don't use this method if images begin to appear on the wall or blackboard to distract you. An alternative

is to imagine a cloud motionless in a clear sky or the still dark waters of a lake.

◆ Initially it will be sufficient to do this for five minutes as our minds are not used to stillness. After a week you should increase it to ten minutes for two weeks and then increase it to fifteen minutes for the fourth week.

◆ By the fifth week you should be able to meditate for twenty minutes which is the maximum necessary for a session. If you do it for longer there is a risk you could become a 'bliss junkie', a state in which some people neglect their responsibilities for the natural high they can get from meditation.

◆ At some point during deep relaxation you will experience a sense of detachment in which you will be aware that consciousness is not limited to your body. In this state you can literally expand your mind at will. Do it. Feel the elasticity of the mind as you extend your awareness either side of your head. Then bring it back to the central focal point in your head, then out again. It will feel as if your head is a balloon which you can blow up and then deflate. This is the first step in being able to project consciousness beyond the body.

of mental energy is thought to be an accumulation of all human experience, thoughts and memories, which we tap into involuntarily when we experience certain phenomena – such as knowing what someone close to us is doing at that moment in another location. With practice this expansion of consciousness can be done at will (see exercise 1 on page 15).

Unfortunately we tend to drown out this still, small voice within by our constant mental chatter and our everyday concerns with our physical and emotional needs. It is only when we quieten the restless active thought processes through meditation or during sleep that we can access the sleeping giant that is our Higher Self (our soul or the essence of our being).

Meditation

Those new to meditation should be reassured that there is no need to feel anxious for any reason. You are not going anywhere, other than inward for greater self-awareness and peace of mind. During this inner journey you are always in control. You are not dabbling in the occult or communicating with spirits. The only spirit with whom you are communicating is your own Higher Self, which is the loving, compassionate, all-knowing source and centre of your being.

Many people take up meditation to enjoy a blissful state of deep relaxation, to attain peace of mind, or improve their sense of well-being, and in so doing benefit from several positive side effects such as increased concentration, clarity of thought, a clearer sense of purpose and greater self-awareness. But beyond this simple passive act of reflection and contemplation there is a point when the restless chatter of the conscious mind is stilled, one attains a sense of detachment from the body and an expansion of consciousness that reveals a hidden aspect to our nature beyond the purely physical.

Exercise 2:
Entering the Light

*As soon as you feel comfortable
with Exercise 1 – sitting silently in
meditation – you can move on to this
one: establishing a connection with the
Higher Self.*

◆ Close your eyes and when you feel
suitably relaxed and the mind is
still imagine a small white spot in
the middle distance. Visualize it
increasing in size and brilliance as
it draws nearer. Watch it coming
closer and closer until it is the
height of a door and you are able
to step into it. Now take a deep
breath and pass through to the
other side. What do you see there?

◆ At first the images may be
indistinct, but they will come
into focus. Perhaps it is a scene
from your past, or an unfamiliar
landscape. If so, enter the scene or
explore the landscape as you would
in a dream.

◆ Do not try to manipulate the
images. Let the imagery develop
spontaneously.

◆ Are there any people? If so, try
to speak with them through your
thoughts. Ask who they are and
if they can help you. They might
have a message for you which
offers the answer to something that
has been troubling you or they may
have some general advice that is of
value to you at this time.

◆ But do not be impatient to find
something of significance. At this
early stage it is sufficient to be able
to sustain the imagery without
effort. Significant symbols will
come with practice.

◆ When you are ready, open up
your eyes and return yourself to
waking consciousness.

Accessing the Unconscious

TASK: VISUALIZATION

Some people find it difficult to visualize and tend to give up too easily. But with practice you will stimulate the Third Eye (the organ of psychic awareness) in the centre of your forehead (initially by meditation and later at will) and the imagery will become more vivid. The task for week one is to sit in silent meditation for five minutes twice a day and imagine a small, coloured bouncing ball against a plain background.

If you can keep this image in your mind without adding anything else to the picture and control the bouncing ball for five minutes you will be ready to move on to the following stage – exploring the landscape of the Unconscious using creative visualizations, which are known as pathworkings.

At this stage you may be asking yourself why you might want to explore the Unconscious if there is a risk of awakening unpleasant, suppressed memories or unleashing your deepest fears. The simple answer is that fear is a stumbling block to both psychic development and self-awareness. By clearing these safely during meditation when you are in complete control you reduce the risk of them erupting in your sleep as nightmares. Furthermore, when you probe the Unconscious during a visualization you do so with detachment, observing the scene as if it was someone else's experience and not your own. This is because in this heightened state of awareness your Higher Self is considering the actions and experience of the lower self or ego. It is the ego that has been hurt or feels vulnerable, not the real you. Of course, if you have a serious trauma to work through it must be done under the supervision of a professional therapist. Only minor fears and phobias can be treated on your own using these exercises.

Exercise 3: The Garden

This visualization guides you safely into the Unconscious, where you can seek guidance from your all-knowing Higher Self, or you can use it for relaxation or relief of stress.

◆ Make yourself comfortable, close your eyes and every time you breathe out say to yourself 'I am calm and centred'. Repeat this until you feel in a deep state of relaxation.

◆ Now remain silent and still as you imagine that you are sitting by an open window in a large country house listening for the sound of birdsong from the garden. It is high summer and you can also hear the drone of bees searching for pollen among the flowers. The scent of sweet peas growing under the window is intoxicating. You want to go outside and lie under the shade of the trees and breathe in the soft, warm scented air.

◆ Visualize yourself rising from the chair and opening the doors leading out onto a balcony overlooking the garden. The sun envelops you in a radiance that seems to soak into your skin and invigorate every cell. There is a short flight of ten steps leading down to the lawn. Descend slowly, saying to yourself as you go, 'Ten ... relax ... Nine ... relax ... Eight ... calm and centred ... Seven ... relaxation ... Six ... going down ... Five ... deeper ... Four ... going down ... Three ... down, deeper ... Two ... deeper ... One ... peace.'

◆ You cross the lawn feeling freer than you have ever felt before. Then you come to a short flight of steps leading down to a sunken garden. As you go down count each step and say to yourself, 'Ten ... down ... Nine ... down ... Eight ... deeper ... Seven ... deeper ... Six ... letting go all fears ... Five ... safe and secure ... Four ... safe ... Three ... and secure ... Two ... safe ... One ... safe.'

◆ You explore the sunken garden and are drawn to a fountain in the centre. There you listen to the bubbling waters and are mesmerized by the reflected, sparkling sunlight on the surface. As you gaze at the light it intensifies, but you can't pull away. A moment later a figure emerges from the light and stands before you. It is your inner guide. Its face is radiant with love, understanding and compassion. It has come to answer your questions and to offer guidance if you need it.

◆ So now ask whatever questions you wish and listen for the answers. They may come as a soft, inner voice or you may be given something that is symbolic of what you need. If you don't receive anything, be patient – the answer may appear in your dreams.

◆ When you are ready, count down slowly from ten to one, open your eyes and return to waking consciousness.

Exercise 4:
The Inner Journey

Initially you may find difficulty distinguishing between a vision that offers you a genuine insight and your imagination. If so, this visualization should help to stimulate spontaneous images from the deeper recesses of the Unconscious.

◆ Place the pathworking cards in their relevant positions on the Tree according to the diagram.

◆ Now select one you feel drawn to. Don't take too long over this. Pick it up and study it. Don't try to interpret the symbolism, just absorb the image.

◆ Keep it in your hand as you close your eyes, retaining the picture in your mind.

◆ When the image is fixed in your mind visualize yourself stepping into the picture. Enter the world of the card and explore it for 10–15 minutes. You may meet the relevant archetype who symbolizes that level of consciousness or you may receive some psychological or spiritual insight.

◆ When the time is right, return to waking consciousness.

Pathworking

Pathworking is an advanced form of guided meditation that offers a symbolic map of the conscious and unconscious mind, known as the Tree of Life, which you can explore to stimulate psychic insight and heighten self-awareness (see diagram). The appearance of the relevant archetype in the scene confirms that you have accessed the desired level of consciousness.

Archetypes of the psyche

Malkut (The Kingdom): A strong, healthy man or woman representing the physical world.

Yesod (The Foundation): A wilful child or an ambitious prince representing self-awareness.

Hod (Reverberation): A receptive and enthusiastic student representing the active aspect of our natural intelligence concerning communication and learning.

Nezah (Eternity): Sensual figures representing the instincts and our preoccupation with pleasure and pain.

Tiferet (Beauty): Reclining figure representing surrender of the ego to the unconditional love of the Higher Self.

Gevurah (Judgement): A learned authority figure representing self-discipline.

Hesed (Mercy): A merciful king representing tolerance, forgiveness and restraint.

Daat (Higher Knowledge): An artist deep in thought representing inspiration and intuition.

Binah (Understanding): A learned, compassionate and patient teacher whose uncommon understanding is the result of long study and reflection.

Hokhmah (Wisdom): A prophet whose glimpse of the greater reality represents wisdom attained through revelation.

Keter (The Crown): An archangel representing the divine aspect of human nature.

Tarot cards are frequently used as a visual aid to access the different levels of consciousness as they symbolize the various complimentary attributes in that region of the psyche. But you do not need to be familiar with the tarot to practise pathworking, although familiarity will make access to the inner landscape easier. Neither is it necessary for you to own a pack of tarot cards to do these exercises. You can make your own pack of pathworking cards by cutting out appropriate pictures from magazines following the descriptions above, or drawing your own. You don't have to be an artist to paint your own cards. In fact, they will be more effective if you have made them yourself as they will express your own inner vision and be charged with your personal energy.

Exercise 5: Exploring the Path of the Psyche

When you feel ready to go deeper into the inner landscape you can experiment with a variation on the previous exercise.

◆ Choose three cards that form a triad (for example, Malkut, Hod and Nezah). Lay them face up in front of you and memorize them in detail.

◆ Then close your eyes and visualize yourself in an unfurnished room such as a temple, chapel or monk's cell, contemplating the first card that has been painted on the door facing you.

◆ When you are ready, enter the door and explore the world beyond in search of the second card which you may find on the entrance to another significant building. The third card will be on a further doorway.

◆ The relationship between the cards and the corresponding attributes in your psyche should become clear. And you may also experience a shift in consciousness when moving from a lower level to a higher state of awareness.

The Secret Self

We are far more complex beings than our physical appearance suggests. Our physical form is merely the outer expression of our True Self which is a matrix of universal energy with the capacity to heal the body and create its own reality. In this section you will learn about the Secret Self that science has still to discover, and learn techniques for manipulating this energy for increased health, healing and psychic exploration. You will be introduced to the chakras and discover how to see and read the aura. There are also techniques for practising psychic healing and for dowsing and divination using a pendulum.

Exercise 1: Grounding
Exercise 2: Centring the Chakras
Exercise 3: Feeling the Auric Field
Exercise 4: Seeing the First Layer of the Aura
Exercise 5: Giving an Auric Reading
Exercise 6: How to Channel Healing Energy
Exercise 7: Treasure Hunt

Visualize yourself seated on a grassy mound overlooking rolling hills and fields. Nestle your back against the trunk of an old oak tree and get a sense of the size and strength embodied in this imposing tree.

◆ Lose your sense of self as you drift deeper into relaxation and become as one with this living expression of the life force. See your legs intertwining with the enormous roots stretching deep into the soil and draw strength from the earth.

◆ Now visualize your arms stretching to the sky and merging with the branches that are reaching heavenward.

◆ Feel the infinite power of the oak as you stretch towards the sun and absorb the light into every cell of your being. Be aware of it blending with the energy that you are drawing up from the earth. Feel the power, strength and security that being a channel for the celestial and terrestrial forces gives you.

◆ When you are ready return to waking consciousness by counting slowly down from ten to one and open your eyes.

The Chakras

What are the chakras?

We are all much more than the physical being we see in the mirror each morning. Our bodies are vehicles for the divine spark of individual consciousness some call the soul which is animated and sustained by the universal life force.

This vital force is known as 'ch'i' by the Chinese, 'prana' by the Hindus and as 'bio-energy' by a growing number of enlightened scientists. It is circulated around the body by seven wheel-like vortices known as chakras and a network of veins known as meridians, which connect our etheric body to its physical counterpart. Both the veins and the vortices are invisible to the naked eye, but they can be seen with the Third Eye (as previously described) of psychic sight and can be felt by simply attuning to the more subtle vibrations in the body (see exercise 2, pages 26–27, and exercise 3, page 28).

The importance of balance

When our emotional balance is disturbed, or if we are under mental stress or succumb to some kind of physical infection, the chakras can become destabilized, disrupting the free flow of the life force and causing the body to manifest symptoms of 'dis-ease'. For this reason it is important to attune yourself to these subtle energy centres prior to carrying out any psychic work. You will also need to be familiar with the specific area of awareness governed by each chakra and its corresponding part

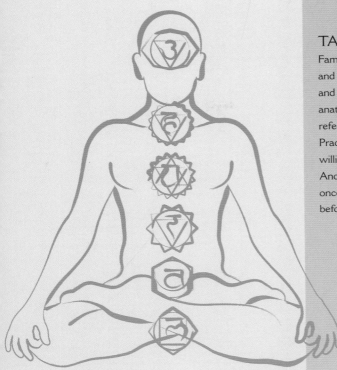

Familiarize yourself with the chakras and memorize the colour sequence and the corresponding parts of the anatomy, so that you don't have to refer to the book when healing. Practise healing on yourself and willing family members and friends. And practise centring the chakras once a day, preferably in the morning before you begin your daily routine.

of the anatomy and with the associated colours for healing purposes (see exercise 2, pages 26–27).

How do they work?

All of the chakras open from front to back, except for the Root chakra, which opens downwards, and the Crown chakra, which opens upwards. The first three chakras are concerned with those psychic abilities that depend upon an emotional rapport with a client (for example, psychometry, auric reading and healing) while the Throat, Third Eye and Crown chakras operate at a higher frequency allowing you to acquire mental abilities such as clairvoyance, clairaudience and communication with discarnate beings, such as your spirit.

Exercise 2: Centring the Chakras

This is an essential exercise for stimulating the chakras and balancing the flow of vital energy throughout the body. The exercise can be performed either standing or sitting.

◆ Close your eyes and breathe deeply from the diaphragm. Begin by visualizing rich, brown soil beneath your feet. Sense the life force rising from the earth, penetrating the soles of your feet and sending vital energy rising up through your calf muscles, into your knees and on into your thighs where it stimulates the **Root chakra** at the base of your spine.

◆ To feel the energy of each chakra place your palm on that area and move it an inch or so away, then back again until you feel a slight pressure as if there is an invisible force-field at that point. As you continue to stimulate the chakra with your hand you should begin to feel a warmth or a tingling sensation.

◆ The **Root** or **Base chakra** governs all forms of physical action, specifically the area of the legs and feet, and is associated with our primal instinct of survival, the 'fight or flight' response. Place your palms on the inside of your thighs and feel the warmth of this energy being absorbed into every cell. At the same time visualize what its associated phrase 'I have' means to you. (Each chakra has an associated phrase, where everything in existence is an expression of the universal laws.) You may discover that you are expending too much energy on unimportant activities, or that you lavish your attention on

others because you under-value yourself. It is through exercises such as this that you will become aware of how the psychological and psychic arts converge.

◆ Now visualize a vivid orange lotus flower emerging from the **Sacral chakra** beneath your navel. Feel the revitalizing power of this chakra surging up into your lower back, chest, arms, hands and fingers as you allow yourself to be absorbed in orange, which is the colour of emotional energy. This chakra governs the reproductive system and sexuality. Its energy is expressed in the phrases 'I feel' and 'I want'. As you contemplate what these words mean to you the images may reveal that an unproductive relationship is draining you of energy, or that you find it difficult making rational decisions because you let anxieties confuse the issue.

◆ Next imagine a vivid yellow lotus flower opening from the **Solar Plexus chakra** a few inches above the navel. This chakra governs the stomach, liver, spleen and digestive system. Its energy is expressed in the phrase 'I can' and is largely concerned with our sense of identity (how we see ourselves), our sense of purpose and our perception of the world that surrounds us. As you sense the energy of this whirling vortex, contemplate how you express the qualities of self-will and determination.

◆ The fourth lotus unfolds its waxy green leaves from the **Heart chakra** in the centre of the

chest. Green is the colour of harmony and of Nature. Stimulating this chakra cultivates compassion and creates a less self-centred perspective of life. Its energy is expressed in the phrase 'I love' and is concerned with relationships and unconditional regard for others in contrast to the basic needs and emotions associated with the lower chakras. Its physical function is to regulate the heart, blood and circulatory system. As you stimulate this chakra repeat the phrase 'I love' and allow the associated imagery to release any suppressed emotions.

◆ The fifth lotus blossoms in a limpid blue from the **Throat chakra**. Blue governs our creativity and our ability to communicate our thoughts and feelings. Its physical function is concerned with speech and the respiratory system. Its energy is expressed in the phrase 'I say'. Visualize being enveloped in blue and see what it reveals about your ability to express yourself to others.

◆ The sixth centre is known as the **Third Eye** or **Brow chakra**. It governs the physical functions of the pituitary and pineal glands

(which regulate our hormonal balance) and is associated with all forms of understanding as well as those psychic abilities concerned with insight and intuition. To test the potential of this chakra visualize a purple lotus opening in the middle of your forehead while contemplating a problem for which you require guidance, and you will receive an inspired answer. Its energy is expressed in the phrase 'I see' and in the ability to visualize and dream.

◆ Finally, focus on the top of your head where a pure white lotus emerges from the **Crown chakra**, bringing spiritual illumination and understanding. This chakra is associated with self-realization and its energy is expressed in the phrase 'I am'.

◆ Now visualize each of these vibrantly coloured lotus flowers aligned along the axis of your spine, balancing and centring the vital energy that maintains your health and sense of well-being. As you do so you sense movement in the **Base chakra** and see a glistening silver serpent arising from the centre. This is the symbol of Kundalini, the power which resides within. Watch as it rises through the chakras, activating each in turn to spin them faster still, and then finally strikes at the Crown bringing illumination and the gift of second sight.

◆ When you are ready, gradually return to waking consciousness by counting down slowly from ten to one and open your eyes.

Exercise 3:
Feeling the Auric Field

The benefits of being able to see the aura (described right) come after you are able to feel it. Once you have proven its existence to yourself you should find it easier to accept the greater reality of which you are an indispensable part.

◆ Place your hands 30 cm (12 in) apart with the palms facing each other and fingers outstretched.

◆ Now bring them together very slowly but don't let them touch.

◆ Pull them apart and bring them together repeatedly, as if you are shaping something soft and elastic like a balloon between your hands. You should be able to feel the subtle energy field from both hands pushing against one another.

◆ If you don't feel anything out of the ordinary at first try making a small circle with one finger around your Third Eye chakra in the centre of your forehead. You should feel a tickling sensation as you stimulate the pineal gland and awaken your psychic senses. Then try bringing your hands together once more as described above.

Have you ever sensed that someone was in a bad mood before they had spoken to you? Perhaps you felt a change in the atmosphere when someone who was intense or antagonistic sat next to you on the bus or train? If you are particularly sensitive you may have felt that they had invaded your 'personal space'. Maybe you have felt exhausted after being in contact with someone who is ill? If so, you are acutely sensitive to the energy field of others, but you need to develop the ability to see as well as feel the aura.

What is it?

The aura is a field of energy surrounding the human body, which can be both seen and felt by those who have attuned to its higher vibrational frequency. It has seven layers, each one emanating from a specific chakra and coloured by the quality of energy in that chakra. The more sensitive you become, the more layers you will be able to see. The first layer is the etheric field which extends a few centimetres around the body. It is the densest level of energy and therefore the first level that you are likely to see when you begin your exploration.

How can it help me?

With practice anyone can develop the ability to read their own aura and that of others. If you can see the various colours surrounding yourself, your friends and your family, you will be able to diagnose their physical, emotional, mental and spiritual state to identify the source of any problems, even if they don't feel like talking about it. And you may have advance warning of illness before physical symptoms appear. You will also be able to protect yourself so that you are not easily disturbed by other people's moods, nor unintentionally drained of energy by those who are ill. If you work in a stressful environment or are a carer and regularly come into contact with people who are ill, you will be able to do your job more efficiently and still have enough energy at the end of the day.

Exercise 4: Seeing the First Layer of the Aura

We are all able to see the aura, but unless you are a gifted psychic you will need to train yourself to tune in to its subtle energy.

◆ Breathe deeply and steadily. When you feel suitably relaxed extend one hand with the palm downwards at a comfortable distance, as if you were reading a book or magazine. Ideally the lighting should be low and your hand placed in front of a plain background, preferably white. For best results try resting your hand on a table that has been cleared of any objects that might distract you.

◆ Now soften your gaze until you are looking past your hand to the surface of the table or, if you are holding your hand out in front of you, to a point in the middle distance.

◆ After a few minutes you should begin to see a fine outline of electric blue light surrounding your fingers. See if you can sustain this soft focus for a few minutes and then look at your other hand.

The Evidence

Scientific proof of the existence of the aura has been supplied by a technique known as Kirlian photography, which involves a specially adapted camera and film that are sensitive to electromagnetic radiation. You can have your own aura photographed using this technique at many of the psychic fairs that can be found around the country. In a series of tests at the Neuropsychiatric Institute at UCLA (the University of California, Los Angeles, USA) Kirlian photography recorded energy radiating from the fingertips of psychic healers. Subsequent experiments revealed that all living things have their own aura, even trees and plants. Leaves which had been torn at one corner still emitted energy around the missing portion. This might explain the medical condition known as 'phantom limbs' in which amputees complain that they can still feel their missing limbs.

What next?

Ask a friend or family member to stand in the centre of the room with their eyes closed. Then put your hand a few centimetres from one of the seven key chakra points and ask them to identify where you have penetrated their aura. Then change round and ask them to experiment with you in the same way. You should feel an almost physical presence at that point even though they are not touching you. Finally, ask them to sit opposite to you so that you can 'tune in' to them and see the aura all around their body. But ask them to close their eyes so that they don't look at you and risk distracting you. You should see the same electric blue outline around your friend.

The colours of the aura and their significance

Red: vital energy, an active person.
Dark red: anger.
Orange: optimism and confidence.
Pale orange: low self-esteem, indecisiveness.
Yellow: openness.
Pale yellow: withdrawal.
Green: an emotionally well-balanced individual.
Pale green: lack of commitment.
Murky green: emotional conflict, dependency or possessiveness.
Blue: a calm, centred personality.
Murky or pale blue: sadness.
Purple: an intuitive, spiritually-aware person.
Murky purple: a tendency to self-deception and idle daydreaming.
White: spiritual awareness, inner strength and serenity. This is the origin of the halo in spiritual art.

Exercise 5: Giving an Auric Reading

The real test of emerging psychic sensitivity is to give a reading to a stranger. This exercise explains how to do so effectively and sensitively. The human aura is constantly changing to reflect our mental, emotional and psychological states. So when giving a reading you must ensure that the sitter knows that what you describe is your impression of what their aura reveals at the present moment. You must never make a diagnosis. If you feel something is seriously wrong you should tactfully advise them to seek professional medical advice, but never in a manner that might alarm them.

◆ Sit opposite your client and begin by relaxing into a meditative state. Then work through the chakras beginning with the Root chakra. Stimulate it as previously described and project that energy outwards to the corresponding point in your client's body. What impressions do you have?

◆ You may sense emotion or see a colour, a symbol or an image from their life that has impressed itself in the aura. If the colour is muddied or indistinct this could indicate a problem which you can then probe by asking your guides or Higher Self for more information, or by visualizing yourself absorbed in that colour.

◆ Be open, don't analyse it with your intellect, or interpret it but instead trust your intuition to reveal what you need to know. And as you get these impressions describe them to the sitter. Let them draw the right conclusions from the information you give them.

◆ If you see what you think is an image of a future event, resist the temptation to make a prediction. You might just be picking up on their desire to achieve something. In time you will learn to distinguish between these impressions.

Mind Energy

Yugoslavian healer Tamara Mount is one of the most powerful and perceptive psychics with whom I have had the pleasure of working. Her experiences reveal much about the nature of personal energy and its potential to create or cure disease.

Open your mind to energy

'If you want to raise your awareness to levels beyond the mundane or material world you have to overcome your fear of encountering different energy forms. You have to be open if you want to be intuitive. If you keep analysing, quantifying and questioning everything, you'll be filtering your impressions through your intellect instead of your feelings and you can only experience energy with your feelings.

I first experienced the various energy levels as colours. One day I was looking in the mirror and I saw my own aura. It just appeared spontaneously. It was a brilliant lime green. Then I started to explore the different layers with my hand. First at arm's length and then I'd bring my palm in closer to sense the distinctive density of each individual layer. Many so-called incidents of spirit manifestation is simply energy seeking to be grounded just like lightning. I see them as channels of celestial energy which revitalize the earth and preserve the eco system. A friend once called me in to clear her shop of a smoky black apparition which she thought was a ghost, but I could see it was one of these clouds of charged particles. So I stood in the middle of it and allowed it to use me as a channel to the earth. It's easy to distinguish between energy and a ghost. When you are in the vicinity of a ghost you can sense a presence and you get impressions of the personality or consciousness behind it.'

What can energy do?

'Everything is an expression of Universal energy. It's my understanding that angels and spirit guides are the embodiment of a finer form of energy, not conscious entities. And that's why they appear in such a clichéd form because that is the way we are conditioned to perceive them. We are all beings of energy in a physical shell and the most powerful energy is our thoughts. Mental energy can create our own heaven and hell. I've seen electric sparks around the throat of someone who was angry and I can sense the harm they are doing to themselves and those they are sending it to. If this energy is not channelled it can manifest as physical illness. People can literally eat themselves up with resentment and frustration. Disease always has a psychic or psychological cause. That's why some people can smoke heavily all their lives and not develop lung cancer while others can contract the illness even though they've never smoked.

Consciousness doesn't just reside in the mind. Our experiences are stored in every cell. They hold not only a visual impression but also the feeling associated with a particular experience. And that's why we need to clear potentially destructive residues. When I give healing I experience the energy associated with that part of the anatomy. I might also get a specific smell and a taste in my mouth which gives me another clue as to the cause of the problem. For example, if the person has a digestive disorder I might get a bitter taste in my mouth and scent an acidic odour as if I was manifesting the same symptoms.

We all need to be psychically sensitive because we must become acutely self-aware. Otherwise we can't evolve and that's the whole purpose of existence. When you have developed your psychic senses you can access a level where thoughts exist before they manifest in action or as symptoms. Psychics can help people to help themselves by bringing problematic issues to their conscious mind. But we can't make choices for them.'

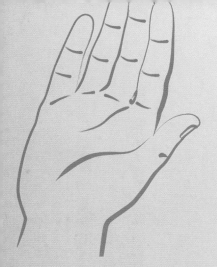

Psychic Healing

I have personally experienced the benefits of psychic healing on several occasions and have practised it on others who have confirmed its many benefits.

Healing hands

Some years ago I had a chronic back complaint cured in a matter of a few moments by a healer who put their hand at the base of my spine. I felt a sense of weightlessness as if I had been lifted out of my body while an adjustment was made to correct the problem. Then I became aware of my body as I settled back into it. The crippling pain I had experienced for over a year never returned. When I had the chance to practise healing on other people they would often comment on the heat that they felt emanating from my hands and the sense of being cleansed and revitalized after the session. If there was another psychic present they would occasionally see and describe to me the spirit guides that they saw helping me and during one treatment I felt invisible hands under my own which had an elasticity like a balloon.

You may think that such an experience might be unsettling, but in a healing environment it is uplifting to be assisted by spirit guides. Such experiences help to dispel our fear of the unknown.

A Modern Miracle?

An elderly friend of mine was diagnosed with pancreatic cancer. The doctors had given him just six weeks to live, but they were so impressed by his determination to be cured that they agreed to try surgery despite a 1 in 100 chance of survival. For several weeks prior to the operation and for several weeks during his recuperation my friend had psychic healing rather than chemotherapy. Initially he felt too ill to travel to the healer, but with each treatment he became progressively stronger. A month after the surgery all trace of the cancerous cells had disappeared, prompting the medical team to visit their patient at home to ask how he had done it. Within a month he was taking long walks and completed a healing course so that he could treat others.

Exercise 6: How to Channel Healing Energy

Healing is one of the highest forms of psychic gifts, but also one of the simplest and easiest to develop. This exercise describes how everyone can develop this ability. Although some people have a natural capacity for healing it's very simple for anyone to channel the Universal life force to treat themselves, or to pass it on to someone who needs it. But if you are going to practise healing you must ensure that you do not inadvertently drain yourself of vital energy in your enthusiasm to help others. So do the grounding exercise described on page 24 before you begin.

◆ If you are healing someone else have them sit on a stool or an open-backed chair so that you can lay your hands on their shoulders, back and spine. Stand behind them and ask them to close their eyes and relax. Whoever you are treating you must respect their wishes if they do not want to be touched. You do not have to make physical contact to transfer energy as it can be absorbed through the aura, although you may find it helps to lay hands on their shoulders initially to establish a connection.

◆ When you are ready close your eyes, take a few deep breaths and relax. Visualize yourself as a clear and effective channel for the Universal energy which you draw down through the crown of your head in the form of a lightning bolt, or you may respond more effectively to the image of a radiant sphere of divine light. Red is a good colour to visualize if you want to revitalize someone who is recuperating after a long illness or who is suffering from ME (myalgic encephalitis – chronic fatigue syndrome), while blue is a calming colour for stress-related disorders.

◆ Absorb the energy into your body and see it coursing through your hands into the body of your patient. Do not try too hard. You do not need to force the energy through by will power. You need to be open and let the Universal life force flow through you to where it is needed.

◆ Once you are grounded and have established an empathy with the other person you can search for the source of their symptoms by making a pass with your hands a few centimetres from their body. Energy blockages will be sensed as cold spots while other problems may be identified by imagery in your mind.

◆ But remember, you are not qualified to make a diagnosis. You are under an obligation to remind the patient that they should always seek professional medical advice.

TASK:
MAKE A SACRED SPACE

If you want to make steady progress in psychic development you will need to set aside an allotted time every day to work through the various exercises. You can encourage the habit by dedicating a corner of your bedroom for healing and meditation, or better still using a spare room if you have one. In time this area will become charged with positive mental energy and a sense of serenity which you will be able to draw upon when you need to recharge your batteries to practise healing or work through the visualizations.

Here are some practical tips for creating your own sacred space:

◆ Be selective in choosing inspirational objects, ornaments and pictures. Clutter is not conducive to concentration and can prove a distraction. A single central object such as a statuette of Buddha or Jesus, a picture of an angel or a large crystal should be your focus.

◆ It might be helpful to have a reminder of the primary principles governing the universe in the form of two candlesticks, representing form and force, male and female, active and passive and so on, with the four elements represented by appropriate objects. A plant could symbolize

Earth and it would also be a reminder of the eternal cycle of growth, death and rebirth in the natural world; incense could represent Air; a single coloured candle could symbolize Fire and a bowl of water could represent Water. But remember, if you use candles or incense the room should be well-ventilated as these consume oxygen and can lead to drowsiness and headaches.

◆ A cassette or a CD player could create the right atmosphere and make it easier for you to sit for long periods of time in meditation by providing appropriate music, natural sounds or replaying the instructions for pathworking visualizations.

◆ Whatever room you dedicate to meditation you will need to ensure your peace and privacy. So, if necessary, you could pin a note to the door of this room to let the other people in the house or apartment know that this is to be a time when you are not to be disturbed.

Extending Your Awareness

Pendulum power

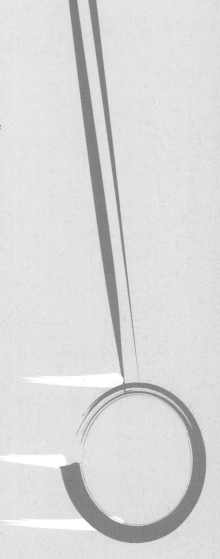

During the 1980s Professor Hans-Dieter Betz of Munich University accompanied dowser Hans Schroter in his search for water in a semi-arid region of Sri Lanka. Betz witnessed Schroter using little more than his instinct to successfully locate 691 sources of water, some of which were 70 metres (230 ft) below the surface in conditions where the normal failure rate could be expected to be more than 50 per cent. Schroter's accuracy rating was 96 per cent. As a result 350 villages were given access to fresh water and at a fraction of the cost that would have been incurred had they piped it from the nearest river.

Dowsing is one of the oldest intuitive talents that we have. Our ancestors are believed to have used it to locate underground streams and identify sacred sites where the Earth's magnetic energy could be harnessed for magical purposes and fertility rites. Today people are still using forked hazel twigs or wire to amplify their inner electro-biological antennae in the search for hidden water pipes and buried treasure. But the most practical tool for the modern dowser is a pendulum made either of crystal or wood. The following pages show you how you can use a pendulum for healing, dowsing and divination.

TASK: TEST YOURSELF

Collect a variety of objects from around your home and see if you can sense the different frequencies characteristic of each using your pendulum. Then closing your eyes, try to identify a flower from a stone, a crystal from a key and so on.

Cleansing your pendulum

Before using your pendulum for the first time cleanse it by holding it under cold running water for ten seconds, then dry it with a clean tissue. You should not let anyone else use it, but if you do you will need to cleanse it before you use it again yourself.

Charging it with personal energy

Before you can use your pendulum for divination you will need to charge it with your own personal energy, as it is acting as an extension of your natural internal radar, so to speak. It is an antenna. The pendulum itself has no power of its own.

Pick it up by the chain using the thumb and index finger of the hand with which you write. If you are right-handed hold it a few centimetres over your left palm and if you are left-handed hold it over your right palm. Now mentally ask the pendulum to indicate 'yes'. It will begin to swing gently from side to side and then make a circular motion which will increase the longer you hold it. To confirm the direction it has indicated, stop it swinging and ask it to indicate 'no'. It will now begin to circle in the opposite direction.

Healing

You can use the pendulum for diagnosing illness in yourself and others, although you must never make your findings known to a patient. You can tell them that you believe you have identified a problem in a particular part of the body and treat them to improve the circulation of energy or to give pain relief, but you must never verbalize your thoughts. It is unethical for healers to make a diagnosis. You must always advise them to a consult a medical professional.

When using a pendulum for healing you will need to ask it to identify energy blockages, areas of discomfort or malfunctioning organs by circling in the same direction as it would to indicate 'no' (usually anti-clockwise). Or you may find that your pendulum ceases to move at all when placed near a problem area which you can then confirm by placing your hand at the same point and sensing for a cold spot.

Divination

Clear your mind using a basic meditation (such as that on page 18) so you don't unduly influence the answer. Then having identified which direction the pendulum will swing to indicate 'yes' and 'no' you can ask it a closed question (a question requiring a 'yes' or 'no' answer) and receive a definite answer, although remember to always confirm the answer by rephrasing the question or asking a supplementary question. Alternatively, hold the pendulum over a map and ask it where you will live or work in the future. You can even use this method to choose the best university for you or the ideal location for your next holiday.

Dowsing

You can locate lost items by clearing your mind then asking the pendulum where the object is using 'yes' or 'no' answers to narrow the search area. You can also locate lost or valuable items by placing the pendulum over a map of the area you intend to search.

Exercise 7: Treasure Hunt

Test the power of the pendulum using this exercise.

◆ Choose a small object and attune the pendulum to its vibration by holding the pendulum over it and lengthening the string until it begins to swing. Using it at this length, you will be able to distinguish between the object you seek and other buried or hidden items during the search.

◆ Ask a friend to hide the item in a neutral space (on its own away from similar objects whose vibrations might confuse the pendulum, and from electrical appliances whose magnetic field might disturb the pendulum). Take your time and move around the area you are searching slowly asking the pendulum to indicate the location of the object.

◆ Ask your partner to choose an item and hold it for a few minutes before hiding it in a container with other objects. Tune into their frequency range by holding the pendulum over the palm. Then pick out each item in turn and hold the pendulum over it asking 'Is this the item X has been holding?'.

Dream Workshop

Contrary to popular belief our dreams are much more than a random recycling of impressions from daily life. This section reveals that in the deepest levels of sleep our dreams can reveal the source of our fears and also offer significant insights into our personality and the reason why we hold certain attitudes that might be preventing us from fulfilling our ambitions. Using the techniques described in the following pages you will be able to improve your dream recall, discover the significance of dream imagery, influence the outcome of your dreams and even access other realities.

Exercise 1: Inducing a Dream
Exercise 2: Improving Dream Recall
Exercise 3: Create your own Dreams
Exercise 4: Dialogue with your Dreams
Exercise 5: Keeping a Dream Journal
Exercise 6: Triggering a Lucid Dream
Exercise 7: The Cloud
Exercise 8: The Astral Visit

Door to the Unconscious

'If (individuals) do not puzzle out their identity and the direction of their lives by the aid of their dreams then they may be brought ... into some crisis which requires that they come to terms with themselves'.

Edgar Cayce on Dreams

Many people consider their dreams to be no more than a jumble of meaningless images while some claim that they don't dream at all. Scientists, however, have identified the brain-wave patterns characteristic of the dream state and shown them to be common in every one of the sample subjects under study, proving that we all dream for at least a few minutes every night, even if we can't recall our dreams when we wake. Jungian psychoanalysts argue that dreams can reveal our secret hopes and fears and are necessary for the integration of the disparate aspects of the self. Psychics go one step further, believing that by taking control of our dreams we can access higher states of consciousness, gaining insight, foresight, guidance and even a glimpse of a greater reality.

The need for dream time

The average person spends eight hours asleep every night of their lives and yet neither the brain nor the body needs such a prolonged period of rest. We continually change position throughout the night to maintain circulation of blood to the limbs, muscles and joints while the brain exhibits sustained bursts of activity which can exceed those during the waking state. So if we don't need eight hours rest, why do we sleep?

It is known that depriving people of sleep for more than a few days can have serious consequences on their mental, emotional and physical well-being. So sleep would appear to be necessary for maintaining our psychological balance, suggesting that we might need a break from 'reality'. During sleep deprivation tests in the 1980s subjects were continually woken just as they entered the dreaming phase and consequently exhibited more severe symptoms than when they were deprived of sleep altogether. When they were finally allowed to go back to sleep they made up for lost dream time by extended periods of dream sleep. Could it be that we sleep because we need to dream? And if so, why are dreams significant?

A different level of consciousness

There is considerable anecdotal evidence to suggest that in deep sleep we can go beyond the purely physiological processing of random thoughts and impressions to a level of consciousness where such phenomena as lucid dreams, precognitive dreams and the so-called 'Great Dreams' of revelationary insight are possible. The following exercises explain how you can induce such dreams at will and improve your dream recall.

Exercise 1: Inducing a Dream

This exercise should help impress the night's images on your mind so that you can make detailed notes on waking.

◆ Lie in bed on your back with your arms loosely by your side and your feet slightly apart.

◆ Close your eyes and regulate your breathing by counting four on the in-breath and four as you slowly exhale, with a pause for a count of two between each breath. After a few moments you will not need to keep counting as you will have established a steady rhythm.

◆ Say to yourself as you inhale, 'Tonight I will dream a pleasant dream' and as you exhale say to yourself, 'Tonight I will learn about myself from my dreams'.

◆ Finally, as you repeat these affirmations visualize yourself standing in front of a closed door. A moment later it opens revealing another in the middle distance. As you approach this door it opens to reveal another and so on. At this point you should drift off into a deep, restful sleep.

The Dream States

The Sleeping Solution

Dreams have frequently offered a solution to many scientific mysteries. After months of mental struggle, the chemist Friedrich von Kekule (1829–96) was able to identify the molecular structure of benzene after interpreting a dream in which he saw snake-like chains of atoms swallowing their tails, the molecular structure of benzene being a closed carbon ring.

A similar dream gave the physicist Niels Bohr (1885–1962) the structure of the atom, while the Nobel Prize-winning chemist Albert Szent-Gyorgyi (1893–1986) was in the habit of assigning his problems to his unconscious mind to provide a solution during sleep. Writers, too, have often been inspired by their dreams. Robert Louis Stevenson literally dreamt up the plot of *The Strange Case of Dr Jekyll And Mr Hyde*, while Graham Greene was in the habit of entrusting his dreams with supplying the next chapter of his current novel.

Most people tend to think that dreams exist at a particular state of consciousness. In fact, scientific research has revealed that the deeper we drift into REM (rapid eye movement) sleep – the state in which dreams occur – the more likely we are to access higher levels of consciousness, each of them distinct from the others.

Some psychics are convinced that during sleep it is possible to contact loved ones who have passed over and that the heavenly realm and the dream state may be at the same level of heightened consciousness.

The physical level

At the lowest level are dreams of a physical nature concerned with instincts and reflexes. Erotic dreams come into this category, as do those concerned with finding food or drink, all of which express a real and immediate need.

The emotional level

Emotional dreams are those in which we dramatize issues which we may not be willing to confront in waking life. For example, a child may dream of watching helplessly as their mother or father walks away, a dream which obviously expresses their fear of being abandoned.

Exercise 2:
Improving Dream Recall

*This nightly review will help to clear
non-essential impressions from your
conscious mind so that you can access
the Unconscious more effectively
without fear of it being cluttered and
confused by irrelevant images. It will
also reduce the risk of nightmares
because it will give you the opportunity
to identify anything that might be
troubling you.*

◆ Before you go to bed make yourself
comfortable in an armchair, close
your eyes and review the events of
the day in reverse order beginning
with this evening. If there is
anything unpleasant, view it with
detachment and let it pass out of
your mind.

◆ Now visualize yourself lying in bed
enjoying a peaceful sleep. See the
hands on your bedside clock

moving through the hours. Through
the curtains clouds can be seen
drifting across the face of the moon
and the stars can be seen shining
brightly as they cross the night sky.

◆ Now visualize the sun coming
up and its warming radiance
illuminating your room.

◆ Finally, see yourself waking up
and recording the details of your
dreams in your bedside diary. Say
to yourself 'I will remember my
dreams' three times. Look at what
you have written in the diary. Now
see yourself writing the words 'I
will remember my dreams' three
times. Then open your eyes.

Exercise 3: Create your own Dreams

If you would like to influence the content of your dreams to solve a problem, or simply to understand how your thoughts can assume symbolic form during sleep, then try this simple exercise.

◆ When you are in bed and ready to go to sleep imagine yourself standing by the side of a moonlit lake. Look into the calm, deep waters and think over your problem with detachment as you would if it was someone else's problem and they had come to you for advice.

◆ If you don't have a problem to solve, think about something for which you would like some insight or guidance.

◆ When you wake in the morning note down the details of your dreams and you should be able to find the answers you seek in symbolic form.

(For more information on symbols see the Dream Dictionary on pages 58–63.)

The mental level

At the mental level are the dreams concerned with processing impressions from the previous day and making associations with past experiences. Such dreams are often highly subjective and can be very revealing about our attitude to life, the image we have of ourselves and others.

The spiritual level

Dreams at the psychic or spiritual level are rare and come when the connection between the mind and body is at its weakest. At this stage consciousness can float free in what is known as the dream body, a subtle matrix of mental energy which drifts in and out of the physical body during the deepest stages of sleep (see page 52). At such moments we may experience flashes of insight that can solve problems which seemed insurmountable during the day or we may have precognitive dreams which foretell future events. In this state it has even been known for quite 'ordinary' people to glimpse the underlying unity of existence in symbolic form, which leaves the individual with a sense of euphoria, although they are then frustrated when they find that language is inadequate to express what they have seen.

A Warning

British psychic artist Sylvia Gainsford describes a precognitive dream that she believes saved her life:

'During my teens I was a boarder at a teaching training college in Brighton and was in the habit of swapping dreams every morning with my room-mate. One morning I told her about the previous night's dream in which our class went on an outing into the town. In the dream we were walking on a rough track through the rain prompting someone to say to a friend of ours, "It's a good job you've got your mac on, Mike". Then a friend of ours, Martin, asked what my friend and I were going to have for our meal that evening. We jokingly replied "Mrs B's eternal soup" which was the name we gave our landlady's soup. At which point a black car suddenly appeared round the corner, mounted the pavement and knocked me down. The dream ended with Martin, who had a connection with the church, standing over me making the sign of the cross and dipping his finger in Mrs B's eternal soup as if it was holy water. It was a surreal ending but very vivid and detailed.

Later that day we went on an outing with the class. It was raining and we found ourselves on the same rough track that I had dreamt about. Someone said, "It's a good job you've got your mac on, Mike", just as they had in the dream and then Martin asked us what we were having for our meal that evening. Before I could reply my friend pulled me back and a moment later a black car came careering out of control round the corner and mounted the pavement. I'm certain I would have been killed had I not told my friend that dream. Fortunately I had described everything in detail to her that morning so I have proof that I dreamt it, but I still can't explain how such foresight is possible.'

Sleeping Prophets

Not all prophetic dreams deal with death and disaster. Celebrated psychic Edgar Cayce (1877–1945), known as 'the Sleeping Prophet' due to his habit of sinking into a sleep-like trance, once prescribed a cure hours before the drug he recommended was discovered! Cayce attributed his uncanny accuracy to his ability to access a stream of collective knowledge which he called the Universal Consciousness.

Cayce refused to profit from his financial forecasts, but Irish peer Lord Kilbraken was not so reluctant. In 1946 he repeatedly dreamt of the names of winning racehorses and won a considerable sum as a result. Lord Kilbraken's claims to precognitive powers were confirmed by his family and friends who all profited from his predictions. Kilbraken had evidently trusted his intuition that the dreams were significant and he acted upon them, thereby strengthening the link with the Unconscious. It appears that we need to make an effort of will to cultivate this sensitivity if the phenomenon is to be repeated.

Exercise 4: Dialogue with your Dreams

One of the most effective methods of establishing contact with the Unconscious, Higher Self or Inner Guide is to enter into a dialogue with the characters in your dreams. But to do so you have to be honest with yourself and let the 'conversation' flow without thinking too much about what you're saying until afterwards.

◆ Close your eyes, take several deep breaths and when you are suitably relaxed visualize yourself returning to the scene of your dream.

◆ Take the part of each of the people in your dream one at a time and speak as you feel they would have done had they had a voice in your dream. Express their mood in your own words and say what you imagine they came to say. You may find that each articulates an aspect of your own personality.

◆ It is not necessary to interpret the meaning of these dreams. What is important is to use the dream to understand how you feel about the situation you imagined, your attitude to the characters and to disclose whatever message they may have for you.

The alpha and beta brain

There is a rational scientific explanation to account for our most vivid dreams and also the existence of all forms of psychic phenomena.

In the 1960s dream researchers proved the existence of two states of brain activity known as alpha and beta which can be identified by their characteristic patterns. When we are awake we operate in the beta state during which electrical activity in the brain produces waves in the range of 13 to 30 cycles per second as we process sensory input from a multitude of sources. But when we dream or meditate the brain wave patterns fall to between 7 and 13 cycles per second which is known as the alpha state and in this state our sensor-filtering system switches off, allowing impressions from the Unconscious and other realities to come through. This explains why psychic experiences are more common when we are relaxed. And it goes some way towards explaining our fear of the dark for it is then that we are more receptive to glimpses of other realities and their inhabitants. Psychics are able to tune in to this altered state of awareness at will while still fully conscious of the world around them, but anyone can train themselves to attain this light trance-like state using meditation or music to achieve a sense of detachment.

The Dream Detective

The most compelling evidence for the existence of precognitive or prophetic dreams is the case of Chris Robinson, known as 'the Dream Detective'. Since the 1990s he has correctly predicted several well-publicized terrorist attacks, including the September 11 attacks on New York, and has often helped Customs officials seize large quantities of illegal drugs having dreamt of flight numbers and seen the suitcases they were hidden in.

Chris has been the subject of several scientific studies including one by Professor Gary Schwartz of the University of Arizona, USA. Each evening Schwartz placed the name of a significant location in a sealed envelope and the next morning he compared it with the detailed description Chris made of the place he had dreamed of that night. In all cases Chris accurately predicted the precise location, prompting Professor Schwartz to admit that he was 'blown away by his accuracy'. Chris later repeated the feat in front of cameras on daytime UK TV. Again his description accurately matched the secret location, prompting the previously sceptical presenters to admit that they were now thoroughly convinced.

Exercise 5: Keeping a Dream Journal

If you want to stimulate your latent psychic sensitivity you will need to trust your intuition and take your dreams seriously. Not all dreams are significant, of course, but you will only be able to distinguish between those that are serious and those that are not if you a keep a daily dream journal so that you can make an accurate record of the imagery and symbols for later analysis.

Keeping a dream diary offers four important benefits:

◆ If you think that you might have dreamt of something before it actually happens, you will be able to go back and check the details and confirm that you have had a precognitive dream.

◆ If you have a lucid dream (one in which you realize that you are dreaming and then take control of the dream) you need to note the scene and sensations the moment you awake, otherwise the rational mind will try to explain it away as the product of your imagination.

◆ If you are fortunate enough to experience a so-called 'Great Dream' of spiritual insight you will need to note every detail on waking as the symbolism will be highly significant (see opposite).

◆ As you become familiar with the significance of dream symbolism (see pages 58–63) you will begin to make connections of your own and come to your own conclusions without having to refer to reference books. This will strengthen your connection with the Unconscious, heighten your psychic sensitivity and you will begin to experience increasingly meaningful dreams.

So, buy a diary with a day to a page and put it by your bed together with a ballpoint or felt-tip pen.

When you wake, immediately make notes of the key events and images of the dream. Doing so will help recall more information before it recedes into the Unconscious. If you write the last episode in great detail you risk losing the fleeting impressions of earlier dreams. You can sketch in the details later using the highlights to jog your memory.

To evaluate your progress so far, take 20 minutes at the end of the first week to read through the entries in your dream journal. Ask yourself, what were the main themes of this week's dreams? What have your dreams revealed about your physical, emotional, mental and spiritual states? Has your dream recall noticeably improved? How many dreams did you recall at the end of the week compared with the first two nights? If you can recall more than two dreams a night in detail you are making considerable progress. If not, be patient. Your powers of recall will improve within a few weeks. What have you learnt about yourself from analysing your dreams? Are you beginning to distinguish between dreams of no consequence and those on a psychological and psychic level? Can you identify those dreams which relate to the physical, emotional, mental and spiritual levels of awareness?

Recording your dreams

It has been said that the most revealing book you will ever read about dreams is the one you write yourself, a comment meant to emphasize the importance of keeping a dream journal.

But the events and images of the dream are not the only important elements. The overall atmosphere of the dream can be highly significant. Unfortunately, this elusive feeling is usually the first aspect of the experience to fade on waking, so make sure that you also note how you felt as well as recording the storyline and symbols. Also try to recall what the characters said to each other, their attitude and their body language as these could offer more clues.

Finally, try to recall any incidents or images during the previous few days that might have influenced the dream and note these down because they may help to explain the more obscure references and meanings.

The Dream Body

Did you ever have a dream in which you became aware that you were dreaming and were then able to manipulate the dream world? Perhaps you found that you could fly and felt that it was more real than a dream? Or maybe you have experienced the sensation of falling just before you awoke and wondered what it could mean? If you were conscious of the fact that you are dreaming, you will have had what is commonly known as an out-of-body experience (OBE) or a lucid dream.

Out-of-body experiences

OBEs are the oldest psychic phenomenon of all. They occur when consciousness is temporarily separated from the body and drifts at will in a matrix of mental or psychic energy known variously as the astral, subtle or dream body. From a number of recent statistical surveys it has been estimated that as many as one person in five in the West has had a conscious out-of-body experience which they can recall in vivid detail.

My own psychic experiences began with OBEs when I was a child and I can still recall the exhilaration of being free of my body and soaring at will over the sea to 'visit' my aunt and grandmother in Ireland. I remember hovering over them and watching them relaxing in their sitting room before returning in what seemed like an instant to my body with a slight jolt. I have experienced OBEs on several subsequent occasions and each time I have been fully conscious that I was outside my body and that I could wander at will or return when ready. It was a state of heightened awareness and of being liberated from the physical constraints of my body and the physical world that was quite distinct from the hazy surreal quality of the dream state. As an adult I have often 'awoken' from a dream to find myself not in my bed but in another part of the house and with that realization I would be snapped back into my body. On one occasion I awoke in the morning and found myself drifting in and out of my body. I could choose to open my eyes or drift off on an astral journey. Unfortunately, anxiety won me over and I didn't take advantage of the opportunity. But each time it has been a pleasurable, liberating sensation and I had no sense that there was anything to fear 'out there'.

Why do they happen?

It is my understanding that everyone has the occasional out-of-body experience, but that the memory of it is usually obscured by subsequent dreams. However, even when we do recall such an experience we tend to deny it, as it is the nature of the rational mind or ego to deny the existence of anything that questions its perception of reality and the physical world in which it has its existence.

Involuntary out-of-body experiences are often triggered by extreme exhaustion, illness, unendurable pain or the use of soporific drugs including general anaesthetic which desensitize the body. However, they can be induced at will.

If you want to experience an OBE try either of the following exercises (see pages 54–55). OBEs will leave you with a different world view and a desire for self-discovery. It should lead to an acceptance of reincarnation and will help you lose the feeling that everything has to be crammed into a single lifetime.

Note

These exercises are designed to improve self-awareness. They should not be attempted while you are under the influence of alcohol or drugs of any kind. Nor should they be practised by anyone who is in a psychologically disturbed state of mind.

Exercise 6: Triggering a Lucid Dream

The purpose of this exercise is to make you aware of the first of the various states of consciousness in which we have our existence and to make you conscious of the reality of the dream body.

◆ Lie on your back in bed and relax into a steady rhythm of breathing. Affirm in words of your own choosing that you are going to enter deep, restful, revitalizing sleep and that you are going to become fully conscious during one of your dreams the moment you see a certain symbol. This could be a door that you will want to enter, a garden that you want to explore or an animal or a person that you expect to meet in the dream. Whatever symbol you choose it should have positive associations.

◆ Before you fall asleep visualize yourself exploring the dream environment after you have seen this sign so that you programme the Unconscious to take this course when the opportunity arises. If, for example, you find yourself in a house, go to the window and look out over the grounds. Then imagine exploring the garden and the landscape beyond it.

◆ It's unlikely that you'll have success on your first attempt so be patient. Practise this exercise each night.

Exercise 7: The Cloud

The following exercise will enable you to leave your physical body at will and explore the astral dimension in your dream body.

- ◆ Lie flat on your back with your arms loosely by your sides and your feet slightly apart. Support your head with a pillow. Now relax.

- ◆ Establish a regular, steady rhythm of breathing and as you do so say three times to yourself, 'I am relaxed and I am at peace.'

- ◆ Now imagine that your body is becoming lighter with every exhalation. It is a pleasant feeling of numbness as you begin to lose awareness of the weight and solidity of your body.

- ◆ With each exhalation sense a cushion of air forming under you until you feel that you can float away on this cloud. Play with the sensation for a few minutes. Feel yourself rising a few centimetres from the floor and then settling down again until you are ready to let go and slip away. You may sense a tickling sensation in the Third Eye centre in the middle of your forehead or a warmth in the Solar Plexus chakra just above the navel. Remember that you are in control

of your experience at all times and can return to your body at will.

- ◆ The first few times that you experiment with projecting consciousness in this way it is advisable to explore your immediate environment – your room and then the rest of your home. Don't wander from your home until you feel comfortable and secure and in full control of your movements.

- ◆ Examine your hands and look at yourself in a mirror. Try to touch everyday objects. You won't be able to but you will be conscious that this is no normal dream. Look back at your body and see if you can see the elasticated silver cord which connects the dream body to its physical shell. It is rare, however, for a person to look back and see the cord, probably because they are normally intent on exploring the sensation and experience.

- ◆ It is not necessary for you to have an OBE for you to become a psychic. If you feel too anxious to try this experiment you can still use the technique for relaxation when you need help to sleep. It will also stimulate dreams at a psychic level in which you will be more receptive to inner guidance.

The aim of this exercise is to obtain proof of your ability to visit other places at will in your dream body. To gain an objective result you need the help of a friend you can trust and whose home is familiar to you.

◆ Ask your friend to put a book of their choice on a chair in their bedroom with the cover face up. They must not tell you what they've chosen and they should not decide which book to use until that evening otherwise it is possible that you will obtain the answer by telepathy instead.

◆ Agree a time for the experiment so that they can be alert at that time and note any changes that occur in the atmosphere.

◆ It is vital that your friend is sympathetic to the idea and will take it seriously otherwise you risk having your own confidence undermined. Again, be patient. It may take several nights to make the breakthrough.

You may not be successful with every exercise – we all have specific talents – but attempting and practising will help you to explore and expand your awareness.

The Dream World

Although the dream body can explore the physical world as an apparition it cannot affect anything solid which is why you will not be able to switch on a light or open a door when you are in this state. The dream body is composed of finer matter than the physical body, which explains why you will be able to drift through walls in this condition. However, the natural environment of the dream body is the astral realm, the non-physical world of our dreams where our thoughts can create an alternative reality. The finer matter of this dimension can be easily manipulated by mental energy which explains the often surreal imagery of our dreams.

Jung and the house of psyche

It is ironic that modern psychoanalysis was partly founded on the insights revealed in a dream. Carl Jung, the Swiss psychologist and psychiatrist, had experienced premonitory dreams from early childhood and was determined to prove his assertion that paranormal phenomena were manifestations of the subconscious, or superior man, struggling to be heard.

While considering how he could do this he fell asleep and dreamt that he was exploring a two-storey house which he did not recognize, but which he knew to be his own. The upper floor comprised a comfortable salon elegantly furnished in a rococco style, but when he descended to the floor below he discovered it was made of bare brick and the furnishings were almost medieval in character. The floor below this was a vaulted chamber that appeared to have been built in Roman times and led down to a cave where he discovered shards of bone and broken pottery discarded by a primitive culture.

'It was plain to me that the house represented a kind of image of the psyche,' he later wrote. 'Consciousness was represented by the salon … The ground floor stood for the first level of the Unconscious … In the cave, I discovered … the world of primitive man within myself – a world which can scarcely be reached or illuminated by consciousness.'

From the images of his dream Jung evolved the concept of the 'Collective Unconscious', a strata of the psyche incorporating memories, instincts and experiences common to all humanity. These patterns, which are inherited, may manifest as dreams or mystical visions often in the form of archetypes – primordial images representing absolutes in the human psyche. Jung concluded that our destiny is to develop to the point where the conscious and unconscious minds are fused, enabling us to channel the wisdom of this 'superior man' at will.

TASK: ANALYSE YOUR DREAM DIARY

Review the entries in your dream diary for this week and underline any significant symbols and characters. Can you eliminate any imagery that was directly influenced by what you had seen on TV or personally experienced this week? From what remains can you identify any recurring themes? Do certain symbols seem more significant in the light of subsequent dreams? Using your increasing knowledge and intuition can you now begin to analyse symbols that are not listed in the dream dictionary?

The Dream Dictionary

Interpret your dreams with this key to the most significant symbols, situations and themes.

Activities

Climbing, walking: ambition. A never-ending climb suggests striving for something unattainable. Ladders usually represent professional or social ambitions, mountain paths are symbolic of a spiritual search for meaning in life, while stairs correspond to our attitude to life. Narrow, steep stairs suggest that we expect difficulties, stairs to the basement represent a willingness to face our fears or suppressed memories.

Digging, searching: the need to probe the Unconscious to recover repressed memories or the search for the Higher Self.

Eating: what we eat and how we eat expresses a hunger for affection.

Flying and falling: an internalization (assimilating the knowledge of this greater reality into your world view) of an out-of-body experience.

Learning: sitting an exam is often symbolic of a fear of having your beliefs tested.

Packing, tidying, clearing out: indicates a readiness for change.

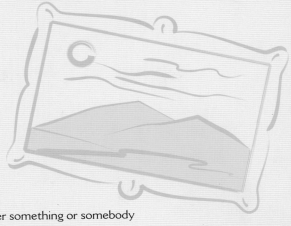

Running: running after something or somebody suggests a fear of loss, being chased indicates an unwillingness to face fears.

Swimming: being carried along by a fast-moving current indicates helplessness, while swimming in calm, warm water symbolizes love and security.

Undressing: in public indicates that the dreamer feels restricted, inhibited, inadequate or insecure.

Death: a symbol of change.

Significant objects

Photographs and paintings: pictures are often self-portraits, revealing either your True Nature or how you perceive yourself at this moment in your life. They can even offer a glimpse of the person you were in a past life.

Money: a symbol of self-worth. Being robbed or losing money would suggest that we feel our efforts are being undermined by others.

Toys: a desire to return to the innocence of childhood and the desire to confide our feelings to someone we can trust.

Keys: symbols of a solution to something that has been troubling us. If the answer is not revealed in the dream itself re-enter the dream in your imagination as soon as you wake up and follow it through to its conclusion or meditate on it using the clues in your dream journal.

Books: memories.

Broken objects: indicate a fear that we are not fulfilling our potential.

Significant situations

Being trapped: a fear of being restricted or overwhelmed by responsibilities and commitments.

Violent argument or fight: an indication of inner conflict and the need to express anger in waking life.

Paralysis, helplessness: indecision and a lack of self-confidence.

Weddings: although this can be purely a wish-fulfilment fantasy it usually suggests that the dreamer is testing his or her attitude towards commitment and responsibility in general.

Party: a symbol of well-being and contentment, although if you are the host and no one has turned up it indicates a fear of being a social outcast or of being disappointed in others.

Travel: one of the most significant recurring themes indicative of our progress through life and our expectations of what lies ahead.

Significant places

Houses: our home, furnishings and possessions express our personality and attitude to the outside world while the house itself represents our current state of mind. If the house is old-fashioned it can be an expression of a conservative nature and concern with one's security and personal comfort. If it is modern then you are more likely to be open to new ideas. But if the exterior is in contrast with the interior it might indicate concern with keeping up a façade to impress other people.

Rooms: dark, cluttered rooms indicate a reluctance to let go of the past, while light, spacious rooms symbolize openness to new ideas and opportunities and a willingness to live in the moment. The attic represents hidden memories; the kitchen and dining room represents our attitude to food which is in turn symbolic of emotional and spiritual nourishment and also our appetite for life; the décor and condition of the living room can reveal our attitude to family, friends and society; a bedroom expresses our need for privacy and personal space, the bathroom and toilet can reveal concerns about our health and cellars symbolize our deepest fears.

High walls and fences: suggest a defensive, mistrustful personality and low boundaries in openness.

Doors: symbolize opportunities. Those that readily open reveal the dreamer's willingness to try new experiences and indicate that they expect little resistance to their plans and ambitions; doors that are heavy or difficult to open indicate a lack of confidence or anticipated difficulties.

Gates: traditionally represent a partner (heavy, stiff gates indicating someone who is resistant to change and small gates a person who is too compliant).

Windows: through the windows we perceive the outside world. A rugged landscape with overcast skies suggests a pessimistic nature and an unwillingness to see obstacles as problems to be overcome.

Gardens: can reveal a lot about our temperament. An overgrown jungle indicates an unwillingness to face problems and a reluctance to deal with unresolved issues, while a neat, formal garden could suggest a conservative nature and a need for order and stability in one's life. A rambling cottage garden or a meadow of wild flowers symbolizes a relaxed, easy-going attitude and a willingness to live in the present moment. The colour of the flowers can also be significant, with vibrant hues symbolizing physical energy, strong emotions and enthusiasm for life, and pastel shades indicating a preoccupation with the intellect and spiritual matters.

Hospitals: symbolize our fear of being controlled or at the mercy of others, especially those with superior knowledge or power.

Libraries: a storehouse of memories and self-knowledge.

Airports, railway stations and coach terminals: suggest that we have come to a point in life where we need to consider who we are, what we really want from life and where we need to go to get it.

Castles: indicate a wary, defensive and insular personality.

Schools, colleges, universities: offer a setting in which we can try to resolve a conflict between what was expected of us in our youth and our achievements to date.

Banks: frequently appear as symbols of authority.

Shops: this is a setting in which we are forced to make a significant choice.

Who's who in your dreams

It is a commonly held belief among those who make a serious study of dreams that each character in a dream represents an aspect of the dreamer's personality, with the obvious exception of people we know in waking life.

Children: can symbolize the innocent, unworldy aspect of ourselves and might appear in scenes involving a search for security or uncovering significant events in our past; a youth expresses our energy and ambitions.

Adults: often symbolize increasing maturity and appear when there are issues of responsibility and commitment to be resolved, while an older person can represent significant changes, particularly those to do with letting go of the past.

Divination

It is a common fallacy that tarot cards, crystal balls and other tools for divination possess the power to enable us to foresee the future. All but a handful of fairground fortune-tellers agree that cards, crystals and runic symbols have no such power. They act merely as a focus for the medium's own psychic sensitivity, stilling the mind and stimulating the Third Eye. In this section you will be introduced to various methods for foretelling the future and increasing self-awareness including tarot cards, runes and the I Ching. You will learn how to use them so that you can prove the validity of divination for yourself and give readings to others with confidence.

Exercise 1: Scrying
Exercise 2: Consulting the Oracle
Exercise 3: Casting the Runes
Exercise 4: Kabbalah Cards
Exercise 5: Three-card Spread for
            Guidance
Exercise 6: The Seven-card Spread

Scrying

Scrying, the art of foretelling future events by gazing into a reflective surface, was practised by initiates of the Mysteries in China, Babylon, Egypt and Greece where seers would use bowls of water, mirrors and even a pool of black ink poured into their palm to induce a light trance.

These days it is unusual to find a psychic who uses a crystal ball. Many prefer to give readings without the theatrical paraphernalia of their predecessors in the belief that such objects are an unnecessary distraction. But divinatory tools such as tarot cards, runes and the I Ching can be of considerable assistance to beginners in developing their natural intuitive powers until they feel confident to give readings without them. They also serve to give the client something to focus on during the reading which helps them to be relaxed and open and therefore easier to read. The real value of crystal balls and tarot cards is their capacity to act as a stimulant for the psychic's intuitive insights into the client's personality, present circumstances and potential. In this sense gifted and empathic psychics can act as spiritual counsellors offering guidance rather than predictions.

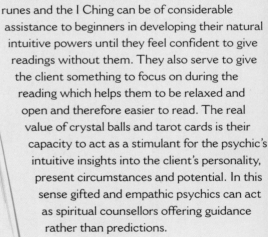
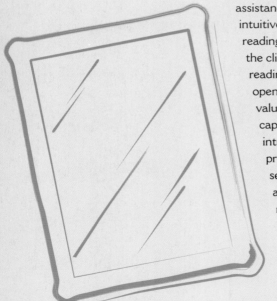

Exercise 1: Scrying

Before you invest a considerable sum in a crystal ball or an inexpensive glass copy, you can experiment with scrying using a coloured glass or brass bowl filled with water.

◆ Place the bowl on a plain surface at waist height on a desk or table.

◆ The room should be dark with a single candle or table lamp for illumination, so that you are not distracted from focusing on the bowl. Ideally, the bowl should be placed in such a way that the light is reflected in the water.

◆ Now take a few deep breaths and relax. Look into the still water and soften your gaze so that you are fixed on a point that is just below the surface.

◆ After a few minutes the water should become obscured by what appear to be clouds. Then they will part and you will be staring into a void from which the images will arise. The images are not in the water, of course; they are in your mind.

◆ If you can remain focused on the images that you are seeing and at the same time be acutely aware of this heightened state of consciousness you should see that the images appear to be mid-way between you and the bowl. This is what is meant by seeing something with the inner eye.

◆ What you see will be for you to interpret according to your own experience and intuition, but traditionally it is said that whatever pictures appear in the left side of the scrying medium concern the present, those to the right side are symbolic, while those to the front and back of the medium reveal events in the future and the past respectively.

Exercise 2: Consulting the Oracle

Consulting the oracle is simple once you understand the rules.

◆ Cast three coins a total of six times and record the number of 'heads' and 'tails' thrown. Heads are drawn as straight horizontal lines (yang) and tails as horizontal broken lines (yin). If, for example, after the first throw there are two heads and one tail, draw a yang line. If the second throw gives two tails and one head, record a yin line. The hexagrams are built from the bottom upwards with the last throw completing the pattern.

◆ To interpret the hexagram you have to consult a list of the 64 possible permutations, each of which has a symbolic meaning. This can be obtained from most bookshops and libraries or even downloaded from the Internet.

◆ The individual lines of each hexagram can also be interpreted, but only when the influence of the adjacent lines indicates that they may be about to transform into their opposites, creating a new hexagram whose significance will qualify the meaning of the first.

I Ching

This ancient oracle is said to reveal the current state of negative and positive forces (yin and yang) in any given situation and then presents the most suitable course of action to create a positive outcome.

It is thought to have originated in 12th-century BCE China with a series of 64 hexagrams accompanied by analytical commentaries which were later added to by the philosopher Confucius. It is said that the Swiss psychoanalyst Carl Jung seized on the I Ching as confirmation of his theory of synchronicity, or 'meaningful coincidences' which help bridge the gap between the conscious and unconscious mind.

Runes

Contrary to popular belief, the runes are not an ancient Nordic alphabet but a composite of Bronze Age symbols, the German runic alphabet and Greek and Latin letters which were widely used on European monuments, ships and artefacts to invoke the protection of the gods. The symbols are ideographic, which means that each represents a significant idea or object. For example, the symbol (Uruz) represents both the sound 'U' and the horned cattle known as auroch, which equates with the qualities of endurance, stubbornness and strength.

The pattern in which the stones fall is also significant. If they form a group it means that they are to be looked at together, but if they are scattered it suggests that there are several issues to be considered.

How do you use them?

They are comparatively simple for the beginner to work with as there are only 24 runic symbols that you need to become familiar with and you can make a set yourself by painting the symbols on smooth pebbles gathered from your own garden, the seashore or bought from a DIY store. These will be infinitely preferable to the plastic variety obtainable from some New Age outlets. The symbols and their meaning can be found in the many books on divination obtainable from most public libraries and bookshops.

Exercise 3: Casting the Runes

◆ Place your runes in a pouch or canvas bag.

◆ Next, formulate a simple question to which the answer will be either 'yes' or 'no'.

◆ Then pick a single rune stone at random from the bag and consult a key to the runes to reveal its significance.

◆ For a more complex question, guidance or insight into a specific problem, choose three stones and place them in a line in front of you.

◆ Reading from left to right the first stone will reveal the truth of the current situation, the second will indicate the action to be taken and the third, the likely outcome.

For more detailed readings nine runes can be cast into a sacred circle marked on card with a felt-tip pen or outside on a paving slab with chalk. Those falling outside the circle or face down are considered irrelevant, while those which land face up but upside down are considered to have a reverse meaning.

Kabbalah

If you are serious about developing your psychic abilities you need a basic understanding of Kabbalah. It offers a context in which such phenomena are possible and reveals the connection between the psychological and psychic aspects of human nature.

Kabbalah is the ancient Jewish metaphysical philosophy at the foundation of the Western esoteric tradition. It seeks to explain our place and purpose in existence through a symbolic diagram called the Tree of Life, on which are arranged the divine attributes manifest in finite form in every human being (see pages 21 and 72). By becoming conscious of these characteristics and bringing them into balance we can integrate both the psychological and psychic aspects of our nature to become fully realized and enlightened beings.

The four worlds

Kabbalah envisages the descent of the Divine in terms of four distinct stages of creation, four interdependent and interpenetrating worlds, each containing the essence of those from which it was generated. These are the worlds of:

- ◆ Emanation (the realm of spirit)
- ◆ Creation (the dimension of thought)
- ◆ Formation (the emotional realm)
- ◆ Action (our physical world).

Kabbalah is concerned with developing a conscious awareness of the upper worlds whilst exercising control over the emotional dimension and maintaining a compassionate detachment from the physical world.

Exercise 4: Kabbalah Cards

You can make a set of Kabbalah cards for meditation, visualizations and psychic insight using a pack of blank postcards and then sticking on appropriate pictures from magazines (see list below), or you can draw your own. Cut rounded corners as this makes them easier to handle.

Once you have your cards, choose the sphere/attribute you would like to explore and place the relevant cards face up in front of you. If, for example, you find it difficult to make decisions because your judgement is often confused by your emotions you will need to explore the qualities of Hod (the intellect) and Nezah (the emotions) in a conscious attempt to reconcile these complimentary aspects.

Malkut *(Image – a house or garden)*: Meditate on this card if you need to be more practical and grounded.

Yesod *(Image – a child)*: Contemplate this aspect if you want to be less self-centred and less dependent on people and possessions.

Hod *(Image – a library or student)*: Close your eyes and visualize this card to increase your concentration, improve your memory and be more receptive to new ideas.

Nezah *(Image – a fairground, party or a hedonistic figure)*: Contemplate this card when you need to get in touch with your sensual nature. Meditating on this aspect can be particularly helpful if you need to resolve guilt issues concerning your sexuality or if you lack confidence or feel self-conscious.

Tiferet *(Image – a spiritual or religious figure such as Jesus, Buddha or a holy man)*: Contemplate this card when you need to practise tolerance, compassion or forgiveness, or if you believe you are being too self-critical.

Hesed *(Image – a kindly maternal figure)*: Contemplate this card when you need guidance or comfort.

Gevurah *(Image – a judge or courtroom scene)*: Contemplate this card when you need to be decisive.

Daat *(Image – a biblical prophet or visionary)*: Contemplate this unmanifest attribute when you are seeking inspiration or wish to develop your intuition.

Binah *(Image – a teacher)*: Contemplate this card when you are looking for insight into a specific problem, or to understand the significance of a difficult situation.

Hokhmah *(Image – a guru)*: Contemplate this card when you seek enlightenment.

Keter *(Image – an angel)*: Contemplate this card when you wish to tune into the divine aspect of your nature for healing and spiritual insight.

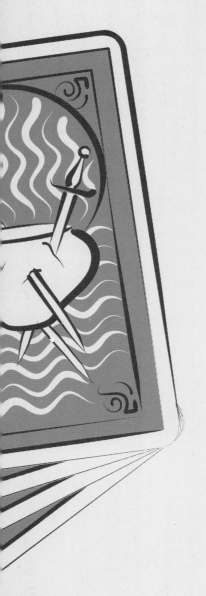

The Tarot

Tarot cards are a proven and practical means of stimulating psychic awareness, although their value as such has been overlooked due to their association with fortune-telling.

What is the tarot?

It is my understanding that the tarot was originally designed by Jewish mystics in the Middle Ages as a visual aid to facilitate exploration of the inner and upper worlds of the Tree of Life in pathworking visualizations and not as a means of divination. That practice appears to have developed after the cards were adopted by the Romany peoples and Christian occultists who were not initiates of the Jewish mystical tradition known as Kabbalah.

Using it with the Tree of Life

The relationship between the tarot cards and the Tree of Life is quite striking. In each tarot pack there are four suits (most commonly called wands, swords, cups and pentacles) corresponding to the four interpenetrating worlds in which we have our existence (spiritual, mental, emotional and physical). Each suit comprises ten cards, one for each sphere on the Tree, which are symbolic of the divine attributes that we all possess, plus a King, Queen, Knight and Page which equate with the four elements (Fire, Air, Water and Earth) that are found in nature and in finite form within ourselves. Fire is equated with our spirit,

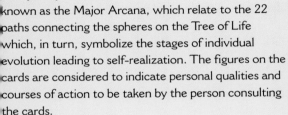

Air is equated with the intellect, Water is equated with the emotions and Earth with the physical body.

In addition there are 22 trumps or picture cards known as the Major Arcana, which relate to the 22 paths connecting the spheres on the Tree of Life which, in turn, symbolize the stages of individual evolution leading to self-realization. The figures on the cards are considered to indicate personal qualities and courses of action to be taken by the person consulting the cards.

Choosing your tarot pack

Traditional tarot cards such as the Rider Waite deck are readily available, inexpensive and comparatively easy to interpret, although you may prefer to choose a pack that appeals to you. I would recommend the 'Tarot of the Old Path' but dissuade you from choosing any pack associated with the notorious occultist Aleister Crowley or practical magic.

Once you have familiarized yourself with the cards and their meanings (which will be found in the accompanying booklet) you can use them to access the inner worlds by visualizing one or more cards in meditation. When you are ready to move on, you will find the following practical exercises very revealing.

Exercise 5: Three-card Spread for Guidance

◆ Separate the 22 Major Arcana cards from the pack and shuffle them thoroughly while repeating a question in your mind. The question should be concise and unambiguous. 'Is it right for me to accept Mr Smith's offer of a job?' or 'Will I be happier if I move to Oxford?' are more likely to produce a definitive answer than 'Should I give up work and look for something better?' or 'Is it a good idea for me to move somewhere else?'.

◆ Take three cards from the top and place them face up in front of you from left to right. Consider all three to give the complete picture.

◆ Select the key words that are relevant to your question and trust your first impressions. Do not be tempted to get too deeply into the significance of the individual symbols.

Exercise 6:
The Seven-card Spread

◆ Using the complete pack, enter
a relaxed, meditative state by
focusing on your breath and ask
for inner guidance in words of
your own choosing.

◆ Shuffle them thoroughly, then
lay the top seven cards face
down from left to right as
indicated below.

◆ Turn one card over at a time
starting from the left. Meditate
on its meaning and record your
thoughts on paper before
turning over the next card.

◆ The first two cards indicate
influences in your life from the
recent past (the past 3–6
months), the third, fourth and
fifth cards relate to your present
circumstances and the last two
indicate possibilities in the near
future. Together the seven cards
cover a period of approximately
one year.

Key to the cards

The Wheel of Fortune: Karma, the universal law of
cause and effect.
The Fool: Free will and self-determination.
The World: Discernment.
The Devil: Self-deception, indulgence, wilfulness and
enslavement.
The Tower: False pride and ill-conceived ambition.
The Lovers: The inner struggle between Power in all
its forms and Love.
The Hanged Man: Self-doubt and indecision.
The Hermit: The search for meaning and purpose in
life, the search for self-awareness.
The Star: The guiding inner light that will lead to self-
knowledge and awareness.
The Sun: The active male aspects of our nature.
The Moon: The intuitive female aspects of our nature
Temperance: The need for restraint and moderation.
If drawn in a reading it can also indicate the need for
forgiveness, decisiveness and self-discipline.
The High Priest and the Priestess: The acquisition of
spiritual knowledge, faith in a positive outcome and
strength of one's convictions leading to Wisdom and
Understanding when balanced with experience. These
cards symbolize the inner growth of the individual.
Death: The need for change to overcome an obstacle
in order to reach a specific goal.
The Magician: The fully realized human being who
has command over the four worlds and the direction
of his/her own life.
The Emperor and Empress: The realization of
potential. Achievement in action (Emperor) or
emotional maturity (Empress).
Judgement: Responsibility.
Justice: Compassion, fairness, mercy.
Chariot: Sense of direction, need for order.
Strength: Self-discipline.

An Unusual Reading

Psychic artist Sylvia Gainsford has illustrated several best-selling tarot packs including 'Tarot of the Old Path', 'Tarot of Northern Shadows' and my own 'Kabbalah Cards'. She believes that the symbolic images can act as a trigger for the reader's intuitive insights:

'When I was asked to illustrate the 'Tarot of the Old Path' I had no previous knowledge of the tarot. The images would come to me in my dreams in full colour so I only had to paint what I'd seen. At other times my brush would take on a life of its own, choosing the colours before I had time to think what I wanted to paint. Later, when I began to give readings I would hear myself describing what the cards revealed before I had time to form the sentence in my mind.

Several years ago I was asked to read the cards for a very nervous young woman. She was so tense when she came to see me that I suggested we sit quietly for a while before we began. I was just holding the cards when I felt a tingling sensation in my skull. It went through my body as if pushed down by an oppressive force. Then it seemed to come under the influence of a greater force which gave it strength for a while before that let go leaving it falling free. It was such a strong feeling that I described it to the lady as it was happening, after which she sat there stunned and said, "you have just described my life". It appears that she had been under the influence of very domineering parents during her childhood and later married a very supportive husband but they parted and she was left to her own devices. When I later did a reading it gave her meaningful and gentle advice which she found very useful and she left me a changed person saying it had been better than a therapy session.'

Guides, Ghosts and Guardian Angels

In the digital age the subject of ghosts, spirit guides and guardian angels might seem an anachronism and yet, there is overwhelming evidence of angelic intervention, spirit messages and ghostly encounters which makes it difficult for even the staunchest sceptic to deny the existence of non-physical beings. It is no longer a question of whether such entities exist, but rather what it is that they signify about the nature of reality. In this section you will discover how to contact your Guardian Angel, how to invoke the angels to protect you and your home and how to communicate safely with your personal spirit guides.

Exercise 1: Making Contact
Exercise 2: Celestial Security
Exercise 3: The Angel's Cloak
Exercise 4: The Angelic Counsellor
Exercise 5: How to See a Ghost
Exercise 6: Conversing with Ghosts

The Angel and the Soldier

In 1946 US Army private Gordon Barrows was so keen to see his family again after years serving abroad that he drove for 18 hours across Wyoming in sub-zero temperatures without a break. By the time he reached the outskirts of Laramie he was in serious danger of falling asleep at the wheel. At that critical moment he noticed a lone hitchhiker dressed in light army denims and pulled over to offer him a lift. But as Barrows wound the window down he saw to his astonishment that the hitchhiker bore an uncanny resemblance to himself. They could have been twins.

Barrows was too exhausted to ask questions or resist when the stranger offered to take the wheel so he slid over to the passenger seat and was soon asleep. When he awoke some hours later Barrows had barely time to thank his companion before the stranger climbed out of the car and disappeared into the desert. Barrows is adamant that he would have frozen to death in the desert had he not been rescued by his spiritual Samaritan.

Angels

In 1987 a German gynaecologist was sitting at the bedside of her dying husband. His illness had been long and painful, leaving her exhausted and emotionally drained. Just at the moment when she felt she could take no more she sensed a gentle hand on her neck guiding her forward and giving her the strength needed to cradle her husband in the last few moments of his life. The fingers of this unseen being were long and radiated a warmth which sustained her until her husband breathed his last.

There are thousands of similar stories which have been reported in recent times, suggesting that angelic encounters are not the exclusive preserve of biblical prophets, saints or mystics.

Many of these individuals had no religious convictions, nor even a passing interest in the paranormal. They cannot explain why they were 'chosen', nor can they fully understand what it was that touched their lives. They only know that they have been transformed by a profound spiritual experience that cannot be conveyed in words alone.

What do angels look like?

These days angels rarely appear adorned with the traditional halo and wings of the past which are now thought to have been simply symbolic of their radiance. Instead, they usually materialize in human form like Good Samaritans and it is only later that those that they have helped begin to question the uncanny coincidence that brought them out of danger

The Library Angel

One of the most striking examples of angelic intervention is the phenomenon known as 'the library angel' in which someone discovers a book they have been seeking under circumstances which defy serendipity (a happy coincidence). The actor Sir Anthony Hopkins had searched the London bookshops in vain for a copy of George Feifer's novel *The Girl From Petrovka* when he discovered an abandoned copy lying on a bench at a station on his way home. Moreover, he later discovered that it was the very copy that had been lost by a friend of his.

The novelist Dame Rebecca West had an equally striking encounter with the library angel while searching for a particular volume on the Nuremberg Trials at the Royal Institute of International Affairs. She pulled out a book at random to prove to the librarian that the cataloguing system was a mess when she realized she had picked the very volume for which she had been looking. Not only that, it had fallen open at the precise page she needed.

Nobody really knows whether an angel is a benign discarnate entity or simply a projection of our own Higher Self.

What is an angel?

One theory states that angels might be a projection from the witness's own Unconscious created by fatigue or stress. For that reason some encounters have been dismissed as typical 'doppelganger hallucinations' (from the German word meaning 'spirit double'), but the clinical definition of the phenomenon only allows for a partial apparition of a ghostly transparency. Dopplegangers do not appear solid and life-like nor do they act independently, as that described in the case of Gordon Barrows (see The Angel and the Soldier, opposite).

A Gift from the Angels?

Angels do not always materialize, but their influence can leave little doubt that a celestial agency and not mere coincidence was at work. An example of this involved an elderly relative of mine who asked the angels to help her find the money to pave her rambling, overgrown garden. By the end of the day she received an unexpected call from a telephone company informing her that quite by chance they had discovered she had been overcharged for 20 years for rental on a second line that she did not have. The cheque she later received was exactly the amount she needed to have her garden landscaped.

Angelic Experiences

It is hard for us to understand why the angelics might intervene to save one life and not another. It is my understanding that they are continuously trying to communicate with us, but few of us listen to the small voice within. Either we distrust our intuition or we are too preoccupied with our own thoughts to hear them. Unless people have a personal experience of the angelics they will find it difficult to believe that they exist, probably because they may not have received a response to their own requests for help. However, esoteric teachings state that the purpose of each life is to learn from experience and we can only do that if we have free will. If we know that every plea for help will bring the angels to rescue us and set things right then we will come to rely on them and cease to function as discriminating and resourceful individuals. However, it is often the case that when a person has done their best and exhausted all possibilities that the assistance will be given unconditionally and with love.

I have taught meditation and psychic development for many years, but the most remarkable response I ever had was for an angel workshop which attracted more than 70 people, many of whom travelled several hours to reach the venue. Most of those who attended that night were in their 20s or early 30s and each had a different experience during the meditations. Some sensed a presence, others felt heat and some saw an intense light or colours. One lady later described how she was taken out of her body into the celestial realms, in the company of two deceased relatives who

appeared beside her and told her that they would
protect and guide her.

Angel meditations

When I began teaching meditation at an adult
education centre I rewrote the angel meditations to
exclude the angelic element, because the course I
was teaching was intended to help people cope with
stress and the spiritual element was not required. But
to my surprise one lady came out of the meditation
in a euphoric state and told the class that she had
experienced an angelic encounter! By following the
guided meditations which I have used to considerable
effect with students over many years I hope that you
too will become aware of the presence of the angels
in your life.

TASK: CLEARING

Before you try to contact your
Guardian Angel you need to identify
any negative attitudes or conditioning
that may stop you from opening up to
angelic influence. Relax with your
eyes closed and allow all thoughts
concerning your attitude to angels to
bubble to the surface of your mind.
Ask yourself 'Do I believe in angels
and if not, why not?', 'What is the
purpose of making contact?' and
'What would I ask for if I made
contact?'. Leave a minute or two
between questions. You may be
surprised by what comes through. For
example, you may deny the existence
of angels, but if so, ask yourself why
you have come this far if you don't
believe in a more elevated plane of
existence than our own. Maybe you
don't consider yourself deserving of
contact. If so, you may be expressing
issues to do with self-worth or of
disappointment that your hopes might
be unfulfilled. If you express anxiety
that you might be opening yourself up
to negative influences (evil entities, or
simply having to hear uncomfortable
truths about yourself) it is likely that
you are articulating an unfounded
fear of the unknown or of losing
self-control. Don't reinforce these
irrational beliefs by acting as if they
have any basis in reality. All of these
self-imposed barriers to your self-
development will evaporate as soon
as you begin work with the angels.

Exercise 1:
Making Contact

◆ Sit with your back straight, close
your eyes and take as deep a breath
as you can. Exhale in a steady
stream, making a prolonged 'F'
sound to expel the last particle
of stale air.

◆ Now visualize an intense white
light emerging from your back until
it creates a halo of vital energy
from the crown of your head to
the base of your spine. Feel the
warmth of this light and imagine
golden wings sprouting from the
centre, the tips reaching over your
head and the bottom touching the
floor. These wings are a symbol of
your immortal, incorruptible divine
nature – your ultimate state of
being once you have broken free
of the cycle of death and rebirth.

◆ Now visualize this beacon of divine
light drawing your Guardian Angel
from the shadows to stand behind
you. Sense its presence and open
yourself to the unconditional love
that it offers you. Feel its gentle,
calming touch as it places its hands
on your shoulders. Ask it whatever
questions you want. You may
need guidance, insight into a
specific problem, protection or
reassurance. Know that it is your
right to ask for and to expect its
help so long as what you ask for is
for your Highest Good and the
Highest Good of all concerned.

◆ When you are ready thank your
Guardian Angel for drawing near
to you and return to normal
waking consciousness.

All in the mind?

The question that you need to consider when you receive a message that could be from the angelics, your guide or the Unconscious is 'How do I know when the contact is genuine and when it is just my imagination?'. The answer is that your conscious mind is judgemental and uses modal verbs, for instance 'should' and 'could'. It will indulge in regrets and self-recrimination, informing you what you should have done in a certain situation and what you must do now. In contrast, your guides, Guardian Angel and Unconscious/Higher Self are loving and compassionate. Their insights are genuinely revealing, their guidance gentle and encouraging, and most remarkable of all their communications come through as a stream of consciousness, the words flowing faster than you can think. You will be genuinely touched and uplifted by contact with the celestials and perhaps even retain an impression of something sacred for days afterwards, whereas your ego will express only self-interest.

Assessing the experience

It is impossible to measure an experience such as the one described above in the same way that you can quantify the results of an experiment into ESP. However, there are means of determining if the contact was genuine. Did you sense an almost physical presence? Were you overwhelmed by its unconditional love which released previously repressed emotions? Did you hear an inner voice or feel a gentle, reassuring touch? Perhaps you felt a warmth in your heart centre or what might have felt like cobwebs on your face. Did you hear the name of your angel pop spontaneously into your mind or did you visualize a radiant figure? Were you given a gift which has a significance for you?

The Angels Within

In *A Book of Angels* the American writer Sophy Burnham recalls a traditional tale that gives an insight into human nature and our relationship with the angels.

She describes how the gods created humankind for their amusement, but first they had to decide where they would hide so that the humans wouldn't find them and spoil the game. If they hid beneath the waves, some would learn to swim to seek their creators in the depths. If they hid on the moon then we would eventually develop rockets and seek them out. Nowhere would be safe so long as man remained insatiably curious about his origins and his purpose in the world.

Finally, the goddess of wisdom came up with the perfect solution. The gods would hide in the hearts of men because that is the one place we would never think of looking for them.

Exercise 2:
Celestial Security

◆ Begin as usual by focusing on the breath. Then when you feel sufficiently relaxed visualize Earth energy in the form of white light being absorbed through the soles of your feet. You may feel a tingling sensation or heat.

◆ Now draw the light up through your body into your lower legs, thighs, lower back and so on, and sense it saturating every cell. By the time it reaches your head your entire body is in a heightened state of awareness and energized from top to toe.

◆ Then draw the celestial energy in the form of a warm, golden light through the crown of your head and visualize the two streams of energy blending in the very centre of your being. Now focus the energy in a sphere of intense light at the Third Eye centre between your brows and project it to the other side of the room where it assumes the form of a winged angel armed with a gleaming sword.

◆ When you have the angelic figure fixed in your mind you will need to empower it. Give it a set of clear instructions to protect your property from those who would wish you ill and for a fixed time limit (for example 'until I awake tomorrow morning' or 'until I return from my holiday on such and such a date').

◆ Then allocate it a significant place in your house, such as the front or back door or the entrance to your property. Acknowledge it when you pass it or when you retire for the night. See it in your mind's eye guarding your home and sense the security that it brings.

◆ When the appointed time comes to end its task, enter a meditative state and visualize drawing your angel back into the room and reabsorb the energy.

Invoking the Angels for Protection

Exercise 2 describes how you can create an angelic thought form to protect your home. I can vouch for the effectiveness of this first visualization, having used it at one time to deter burglars and vandals when I was living in a particularly rough neighbourhood. The houses on either side of mine were fitted with burglar alarms but were continually broken into, the wheels of my neighbours' cars were periodically stolen and their walls and fences vandalized. But thanks to the angelic protection my house remained secure during the entire time that I lived there, while I enjoyed the peace of mind that goes with being in the company of the angels. Moreover, I saved the considerable expense of having to install a burglar and car alarm and the nuisance caused by having them go off for no reason in the middle of the night!

In the unlikely event that an intruder is able to force their way past your protector it could be because you let your guard down, so to speak, by not investing the image with sufficient mental energy. Energy fields are created on the astral level and an unwelcome visitor can barge their way through if sufficiently determined or insensitive to the charge in the atmosphere. But the casual opportunist thief or mindless vandal should feel distinctly uncomfortable when they approach a sacred space, sensing a presence that will be sufficiently strong to dissuade them from entering.

Exercise 3: The Angel's Cloak

◆ Stand up, focus on the breath and visualize a point of white light in the centre of your forehead. Feel it pulsing with energy as it intensifies, eventually extending to envelop your head, neck and shoulders. Now draw it downwards until you are enveloped from crown to toe in a cylinder of light. It seals your aura, preventing even the most negative or aggressive person from penetrating your protection and disturbing you.

◆ Before you leave home in the morning or make the return journey you can appeal to the angels to guard and guide you using the following invocation:

I ask for the guidance and protection of the divine messengers. May Raphael go before me, Gabriel behind me, Michael by my right hand and Uriel by my left hand, whilst above me shines the living presence of the Divine to illumine my true path to my true place in peace.

Now live every moment of the day confident in the belief that you have invoked the highest guidance and protection possible.

Angelic Encounters

TASK: MAKING AN ANGEL LIST

We all have a Guardian Angel in the form of an all-knowing Higher Self and we also have a succession of spirit guides to protect and help us at critical moments in our lives. Some say they even help with the small stuff such as finding a parking place or the right book from a crowded shelf (see page 79). We don't need to be aware of them or even to believe in them to benefit from their gentle guidance, but if we can train ourselves to be more aware of their influence we will be even more receptive to their help. To do so review your life and write down all the times when you have been saved from a difficult situation, whether it was physical danger or a minor worry. Are there more than can be explained by mere coincidence? Can you identify any particular incidents that appear to have been resolved by intervention from an external source?

Although there are numerous credible accounts involving people being plucked from impending danger by unseen hands, more often these celestial messengers will simply offer comfort and reassurance in times of bereavement, despair or distress. Their presence is nearly always accompanied by an aura of unconditional love and compassion which brings even the most cynical person to tears when they recall the incident, even if it is years later. One such incident involved Richard O'Brien, creator of the cult musical *The Rocky Horror Show*.

Richard was alone in his flat suffering severe depression after the failure of his marriage when he suddenly felt two strong invisible arms grasp him from behind and embrace him with such a sense of unconditional love and reassurance that he was moved to tears by the experience. However, later that day he began to doubt that such an extraordinary thing could have occurred when it happened again, as if to confirm that he had not imagined it. Again he was moved to tears by the overwhelming sense of unconditional love emanating from his unseen angel whose message appeared to be that we are never truly alone nor does our suffering go unseen.

Exercise 4: The Angelic Counsellor

When you believe that you have been criticized unfairly or taken for granted and you feel unable to respond you can use this method to clear any residual resentment safely and effectively. Resentment can eat away at our insides creating ill-health, so it must be cleared and our sense of well-being restored.

◆ You will need a pen, paper and an envelope plus a candle, matches and a tin half filled with water.

◆ Make yourself comfortable, then light the candle and work through Exercise 1 (see page 82) to make contact with your Guardian Angel. End the invocation with these or similar words, 'I ask for the blessing of the loving presence of my Holy Guardian Angel so that I might put into its hands this matter and ask that it be resolved for the highest good of all concerned.'

◆ Visualize your Guardian Angel standing behind you as you open your eyes and take up the pen. Now you are ready to write to the person with whom you have the difficulty, describing your feelings and explaining the situation from your point of view. It is as important to tell them how you feel as it is to state your grievance as the primary purpose of this exercise is to clear the emotional bond between you, not to restore your sense of justice. Try to visualize them as you do this to strengthen the psychic bond.

◆ As you write be aware that your angel is looking over your shoulder. This should help you to express yourself succinctly and give you a sense that you have had a sympathetic hearing. In the sacred presence of the angel you should hopefully become aware that the situation was perhaps not as one-sided as you had imagined, that it may have stemmed from a misunderstanding or that you now feel able to 'forgive and forget'.

◆ When you have finished fold and address the envelope (putting a description of the person if you do not know their name) and seal it as if you were going to post it. Then while asking your Guardian Angel to take this message and your feelings with it into the light, burn the envelope in the candle flame and drop it into the water-filled tin. Thank your angel and extinguish the candle. Know that the matter has been given over to the angels – after all they are not named 'the messengers' for nothing!

A final note on appealing for guidance and help of any kind: it is considered good practice to make your appeal three times, once to inform the conscious mind of your intent, the second time to impress its importance upon the Unconscious and the third time for the ears of the angels.

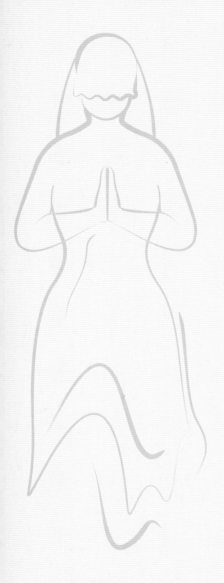

Ghosts and Guides

It is a common mistake to list all apparitions under the heading of 'ghosts'. But ghosts, guides, spirits, thought forms and poltergeists are actually distinctly different phenomena.

What is a ghost?

Ghosts are thought to be a residual impression left in the atmosphere, which is why they never acknowledge the living, whereas discarnate spirits exist in a higher heavenly realm and can only communicate with the living through a medium. They can't do us any physical harm, but if we are unprepared their appearance can prove disturbing – especially if you have a rational mind that can't conceive of there being life after death.

What is a guide?

A guide, in contrast, is the living essence of an evolved soul who has chosen to return periodically to the Earth plane in order to help someone with whom they feel an affinity. Guides are different from angels in that an angel has never been incarnated as a human being, whereas guides did have a previous human existence. Both are benign entities and choose to help humanity from the spirit realm. Guides usually appear to psychics as a Native American or a Chinese man because they consciously take on a form that they know we will associate with healing or wisdom.

Exercise 5: How to See a Ghost

If you live in an old house you can tune into the residual impressions of the previous residents using the following exercise. Otherwise you will need to find a suitable place such as an old church or cemetery where you can sit for an hour or so in comparative peace.

◆ Keeping your eyes open, still the mind by focusing on your breath. Let your thoughts subside so that you settle into a passive state, receptive to the subtle impressions around you.

◆ Begin by making physical contact with the place. Stand with your back to a wall and take several deep breaths. If you are a natural medium you might be able to sense or see something straight away. If not, put your hands on something that will have absorbed an impression, such as a church pew or in the case of a cemetery a headstone. Sit quietly. You may feel cold, heat or a tingling in your fingers. The atmosphere may also change in a subtle but significant way as you become sensitized.

◆ Next, heighten your sense of smell. If you are in a cemetery expand your awareness by centring on the scent of the grass, flowers and the soil. Churches, too, will have retained the smell of incense, flowers and polished wood.

◆ Now raise your awareness to the sounds that surround you and then see if you can go beyond those to the vibrations at the higher frequencies. To do this listen acutely to your watch or a clock. Home in on the ticking to the exclusion of everything else.

◆ Finally, soften your gaze so that any reflected light, such as through a stained glass window or off a polished surface, has a mildly hypnotic effect. Look beyond the light into the middle distance and see if you can detect a shape or figure. If not, look away into a dark corner and see if you can detect any movement in the shadows.

◆ If you are anxious for any reason you can ask your guides or Guardian Angel to draw near, isolating you from any disturbing influences in the atmosphere. You can help the process by stimulating your Third Eye. Simply make gentle, circular movements with your index finger in the centre of your forehead, until you feel a tickling sensation. You are now open to the more subtle impressions in the atmosphere.

Spirits

A spirit is the essence of a deceased person, some of whom may not be aware that they are dead, while others may be bound to the Earth plane because they are troubled. In both cases an experienced psychic can free them from their self-imposed captivity and ease their passage to the next level.

Thought forms

A thought form has no consciousness or personality of its own. It is a man made image created on the astral plane from mental energy and is as insubstantial as a smoke ring. We create them every night in our dreams and whenever we daydream or visualize. We can use this facility to create a mental blueprint to attract what we want in life – which is the real purpose of our imagination – or if we brood on something obsessively we can unwittingly charge it with sufficient mental energy that it will have a life of its own and ultimately it could drain us of our vital energy. This is what happens in cases of addictive behaviour. The creation of such animated images has been a required discipline of Tibetan lamas for centuries, but they learn to animate and control the form and finally to safely reabsorb the energy (see exercise 2 on page 84).

Poltergeist

A poltergeist is commonly thought to be a restless, destructive spirit that is able to hurl objects and physically attack people. However, the evidence suggests that such destructive behaviour is actually the result of the victim's own telekinetic energy being discharged into the atmosphere at times of severe

A Message from the Other Side

Karin Page, founder of the 'Star of The East' spiritual healing centre in Kent and a practising 'sensitive' with a common-sense approach to the paranormal, defines psychic ability as a sensitivity to subtle energies. Karin had been seeing ghosts since the age of six, but it took a message from the 'other side' to convince her to become a medium:

'One day my elderly mother-in-law promised me that she would come back after her death so that I would have proof of the survival of the soul. I didn't take it seriously at the time, but two months after her passing all the clocks in the house started behaving strangely. They all showed a different time and a travelling alarm clock rolled off the shelf and crashed at my feet just as I was telling my daughter about how oddly they were all behaving. Another day the phone jumped off its holder on the wall and started swinging from side to side. Then the electric blanket and toaster switched themselves on. Each time I felt a chill in the air. It was Mary trying to tell me that she was with me.

The final proof came when I went to a spiritualist meeting and was told by a medium, who I'd never met before, that my husband's mother was trying to communicate, that her name was Mary and that she had died of cancer, both of which were true. She just wanted to say thank you for all the time I had looked after her. Then the medium said that Mary sent her love to my husband, my son and his girlfriend and she named them all which left me speechless. The only thing I couldn't understand was when she said, "I'm with Emma now", because I didn't know of an Emma in the family. Mary had never mentioned her. Afterwards I learnt that Emma had been Mary's sister who had died 11 years earlier. Since then I have smelt Mary's talcum powder on many occasions and I know then that she is watching over me.'

A Small but Significant Detail

One of the earliest surveys on the subject of ghosts, *Human Personality and its Survival of Bodily Death* was compiled by a pioneer of psychical research, F W H Myers. It was Myers's conclusion that apparitions were a manifestation of 'persistent personal energy'.

One of the most remarkable and revealing cases that Myers described concerned a travelling salesman who was 'visited' by the spirit of his sister who had died nine years before. The apparition lasted only a few moments and the girl appeared healthy and happy, but the brother was left with a feeling of unease. He noticed a small scratch on her right cheek which he had not seen before. Later, he visited his mother and told her what he had seen. She broke down and described how she had accidentally scratched her daughter's face with her ring while preparing the body for burial. Curiously, the mother died two weeks after the son's visit, which suggests that the purpose of the apparition might have been to encourage him to visit his mother before she too passed away.

emotional and mental stress, which explains why so many cases involve pubescent girls or neurotic adults.

Sensing the spirits

I have sensed the presence of spirits on many occasions, although whether they are family members who have crossed over or guides I cannot tell. When writing on spiritual or psychic matters I often feel what is best described as cobwebs against my face or gentle prods and tugs at my shirt as if they are telling me that they are with me, guiding, inspiring and encouraging me. Sometimes I'll feel a hand laid on my head or something applying light pressure to my ear when I'm watching something on TV or reading about the psychic experience which suggests that spirits are drawn by our thoughts. Many people who have lost loved ones claim to sense their presence when doing something that the deceased enjoyed such as listening to a favourite song, working in the garden, walking in a favourite place or even cooking! So, if you want to connect do something that you know they liked and talk to them while you're doing it – they can hear you. Ask them to reveal their presence by affecting the lights or touching you on the cheek.

Closing down and clearing

It is essential that you desensitize yourself and clear any impressions that you may have absorbed after every session. If you do not you will be hypersensitive to the aura of others and can be influenced by their emotional state. To close down and clear, either take a shower, splash cold water on your face and hands and then stamp your feet to ground yourself, or visualize closing down the chakras one by one from crown to toe.

Exercise 6:
Conversing with Ghosts

◆ For this exercise you will need a photograph of the deceased person and, if possible, one of their personal possessions such as a watch or a ring.

◆ Take the photograph in one hand and the momento in the other. Make yourself comfortable, close your eyes and focus on your breath.

◆ Begin by drawing a circle of soft golden light around you and invoking whatever form of protection you choose in your own words to raise your awareness to a higher level and exclude any unwelcome influences.

◆ Now sensitize yourself to the residual vibrations in the personal object by centring your awareness in that hand. You should feel a warmth or a tingling sensation. If your psychic awareness is becoming more attuned you may even have a vision of the person with whom you want to communicate.

◆ If you don't experience this, open your heart centre by imagining a small pulsating sphere of green light growing in intensity as you go into a deeper state of relaxation. Sense your heart centre softening and envisage the person with whom you would like to communicate emerging from the light.

◆ If that person does not appear you may see your inner guide instead. If so, you can ask it to help you find the person with whom you want to communicate.

◆ However, you may not receive a visual communication. Instead you might have a sense of that person in the room or hear their voice in your inner ear. If it is a lady you may have a scent of their perfume. Do not be surprised if they appear as they were when they were younger or in an idealized form as this is their True Self.

◆ When you are ready to return to waking consciousness, close down, clear the aura and ground yourself using the technique described on the opposite page.

A Glimpse of the Greater Reality

It was not so long ago that all forms of psychic phenomena, and specifically communication with spirits, was considered a very dubious and potentially dangerous practice. However, the current popularity of high profile 'celebrity' mediums such as John Edward, James Van Praagh, Derek Acorah and Colin Fry demonstrates that mediumship is a safe and unique means of connecting the bereaved with their loved ones. It can offer not only undeniable evidence of life after death, but also healing, comfort and closure, allowing the living to stop grieving and get on with their lives. This section offers safe and simple exercises for developing more advanced psychic abilities including remote viewing, psychometry and basic mediumship.

Exercise 1: Test your PSI Rating
Exercise 2: Tuning In
Exercise 3: Personal Impressions
Exercise 4: Reading the Cards
Exercise 5: Seeking Inspiration
Exercise 6: Into the Light

The Stanford Experiments

Since the 1970s several celebrated psychics have subjected themselves to experiments to test the validity of remote viewing under stringent laboratory conditions. One of the most convincing 'subjects' was the New York 'sensitive' Ingo Swann who was able to project his mind to a platform suspended directly above him and correctly identify a series of geometrical shapes. In a subsequent test he was given random latitudinal and longitudinal coordinates by Dr H Puthoff of Stanford Research Institute in California, USA and asked to identify the target by projecting his mind to the secret location.

In 100 separate tests he supplied accurate and detailed descriptions for 43 of the locations which were subsequently verified and 32 descriptions which were correct in many respects. In another experiment Swann homed in on a secret military installation and was able to supply Dr Puthoff with the names of personnel working at the base and the code words for the secret files that were stored there in locked cabinets.

Remote Viewing

I have had many psychic experiences, but the most inexplicable was the occasion I experienced the phenomenon known as remote viewing. Many years ago while attending a psychic awareness group an acquaintance standing in for a teacher placed her hand at the base of my spine, then asked me to close my eyes and describe what I 'saw'. After a few moments I had the image of my own living room but with several significant details 'superimposed', which soon came into sharper focus. I described this other room aloud and in great detail, after which the lady informed me that I had been describing her mother's apartment in New York.

I have no explanation as to how I was able to 'tune in' to a location with which I had no personal connection nor how the lady's thoughts managed to impress themselves upon my mind other than by accepting the possibility that it was a genuine case of remote viewing or a form of mental telepathy. She had no reason to impress me by faking such a thing. She didn't know that I was a writer and she was not even being paid to hold the meeting.

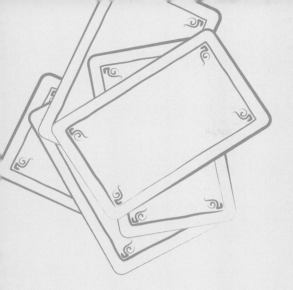

You can experiment with remote viewing yourself. Close your eyes and relax into a meditative state. Let your mind become a blank.

Then visualize a bright light in the far distance as if you were looking at a single star in the night sky. Draw closer to the light until it fills your mind then pass through it and observe what you see on the other side. You may find yourself in a landscape which you can then explore or you may see a single eye staring back at you, unblinking. If so, do not be afraid as this is your own Third Eye, the eye of psychic sight. Its appearance is a sign that you are receptive to impressions from other dimensions and messages from the Unconscious. Their significance may not be obvious at first, so ask for clarification from your Higher Self and feel free to explore the landscape for clues. And don't forget to record the experience for future analysis.

Once you have established this connection do not be surprised if such images and visions begin to appear spontaneously, particularly in the moments before you drift off to sleep at night.

Exercise 1: Test your PSI Rating

You can replicate the Stanford experiments in your own home to test your own PSI rating. All you will need are a pack of ordinary playing cards, although tarot cards would be more suitable as the images are stronger.

◆ Shuffle the pack thoroughly, then remove the top three cards and place them face up on a shelf without looking at them.

◆ Now sit down, close your eyes and enter a meditative state. Visualize the room as vividly as you can. Expand your awareness by sensitizing your hearing, touch and smell (as described in exercise 5 on page 89). Now explore the room with your mind, projecting your awareness towards the shelf. Don't simply imagine that you are there. Be there.

◆ Now rise above the floor and look down on the cards. What do you see? When you are centred back in your body write down the name of the three cards and then check to see how accurate you have been.

America's Psychic Spy

Following my own personal experience with remote viewing I interviewed US Army Major David Morehouse who had been one of the first psychics recruited into America's top-secret psychic spy programme, code-named 'Stargate'.

'Remote viewing is a projection of consciousness involving the opening of conduits into the time–space continuum. With the given co-ordinates fixed in our minds we would enter an altered state of consciousness similar to that attained in deep meditation, before projecting ourselves into the ether.

The separation from the physical body always began with a sound like ripping Velcro and then we would find ourselves suspended in the darkness of space gazing down on planet Earth. Moments later we descended through a tunnel at increasing speed with the surrounding stars blurring into streaks of light until we struck a membrane-like substance which indicated that we had contact with the ground.

We had been systematically exposed to negative locations such as the ovens at Auschwitz for the purpose of sensitizing ourselves to these vibrations so that we would recognize them when we were sent in to probe for the location of a secret police HQ or forced-labour camp, for example. But our data was always collated with information taken from many other sources including satellite scans and human reconnaissance etc. The fact is that remote viewing is not one hundred per cent accurate and it never will be. Much of what is in the ether does not fit into everyday experience so the conscious mind can't compute it, so to speak. Therefore it adds lots of other data from its own memory so that we can accept it as "real", a process we called "analytical overlay". Initially the top brass said that if it proved to be only five per cent accurate then it would be of value, but I know it has often proved to run at around eighty per cent accuracy and sometimes even more.'

Extra-sensory Perception

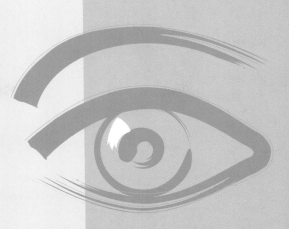

Extrasensory perception (ESP) is an umbrella term for those psychic abilities that are an extension of our physical senses.

Seeing things

Clairvoyance is the ability to see through physical barriers to other locations, a talent commonly known as remote viewing (see pages 96–97), and beyond to non-physical dimensions (see pathworking pages 20–21). A couple of years ago I was given a demonstration of long-distance clairvoyance while being interviewed on a radio talk show. The resident psychic who was broadcasting from another studio in Florida tuned in to a succession of listeners who were in London using the phone line and revealed personal details which they subsequently confirmed. The purpose of the demonstration was not to impress us but to give guidance to the listeners concerning their personal lives and their choices of career. All of them concluded the call by acknowledging that the advice was very specific to their situation and extremely helpful to them.

TASK: TUNE IN TO A VISUAL MESSAGE

The next time you are talking to a friend or family member on the phone see if you can tune in to them and pick up a visual image. Make a note of what you see them wearing and any specific details concerning the room they are in, then at the end of the conversation tell them of the experiment and ask them to confirm your impressions.

Hearing things

Clairaudience is the rare ability to hear the voice of spirit guides and those who are no longer living in the physical dimension, for the purpose of giving guidance to other people. It is not to be confused with hearing the voice of your own inner guide or Higher Self. I witnessed a convincing demonstration of clairaudience while being interviewed on a TV talk show in 1999 and was profoundly impressed. The psychic Derek Acorah revealed personal details about members of the audience which they confirmed. He then went on to give advice concerning their careers and personal plans which they also confirmed were accurate and helpful, although they had not spoken about themselves. During the session he was sitting with his head to one side as if listening to someone who was whispering in his ear and every minute or so he would break off from talking to the audience to catch the next piece of information from his spirit guides.

Sensing things

Clairsentience is the ability to sense the presence of discarnate beings such as ghosts, spirit guides and angels (see previous chapter).

Their presence may be accompanied by a subtle change in the atmosphere, a draught of cold air, a tingling in the skin or a scent associated with the deceased. Female spirits may inform you of their presence with a hint of their favourite perfume or a smell associated with something that they enjoyed doing such as the aroma of freshly baked bread. Male spirits, particularly older men, have been known to announce their presence with a waft of their favourite tobacco.

Sensing the Guiding Spirit

Psychic Jill Nash believes that the job of a psychic is to provide evidence of survival on the other side to give comfort to those left behind and to encourage them to continue with their lives in the knowledge that separation from their loved ones is only temporary:

'Initially I talk to spirit in my mind and ask for their help. I feel their presence and can sense if they are male or female, but I never see them. I'm not communicating with the dead because no body ever dies. They are the same personalities that they were in life. They are simply discarnate. I ask them to give me names and details that only the client will know as validation which helps the client to relax and open up. Then I close my eyes and visualize drawing that person closer so that I am absorbed into their aura. When I make the connection I get excited. It's like having a present that you can't wait to open. At that point I usually feel a warmth and I might see a colour or a letter, or a combination of letters. If, for example, I see them surrounded by blue I will know it is a communication issue and I'll ask them if they know of anyone whose name begins with the letter I've seen or a place beginning with that letter that has a significance for them. That's the starting point. It's an entirely intuitive, automatic process. It's like picking at a strand in a ball of wool. It unravels slowly. When spirit has something to add it impresses itself in my mind. I only receive what spirit wants me to have at that time. It wouldn't help me or the client to know all the answers. We would stop working things out for ourselves and would only put an effort into something that would guarantee to reward our efforts. Spirit says that life is to be experienced, not simply acted out from a script.'

Basic Mediumship

Giving readings for friends and family can be fun, but they are not a true test of your talents as knowledge of those close to you can unconsciously influence your impressions. The real work begins when you give your first readings for a stranger.

Finding a client

The best place to start is at a psychic development or meditation group where you will find plenty of suitable subjects. Such groups can usually be found through the local papers and charge only a nominal entrance fee to cover the cost of hiring the room. They attract many like-minded people who will be supportive and willing to let a newcomer practise on them. And most groups make it a rule that there is no pressure on anyone to 'perform'. However, if you are not keen on joining a group, all you have to do to ensure a stream of suitable subjects is to let your friends, family and work colleagues know that you are giving readings for free. Even the most sceptical will not be able to keep their curiosity in check so buy a diary to make sure that you don't double-book!

Setting the Scene

Before your client arrives, work through the grounding exercise on page 24. Then, ask for guidance from your guides, Guardian Angel or Higher Self and affirm that what you receive is to be for the Highest Good of all concerned. It is important that you remind yourself that you are not seeking to impress anyone with your abilities or prove the existence of psychic sensitivity.

The reading

Once you have made your client comfortable and thanked them for giving you their time put them at their ease by letting them know that you are a beginner. Be honest. Tell them that you hope to be able to offer insights into their past, their personality and the possibilities that lie ahead of them, but that you are not in the business of making predictions and that the impressions are open to interpretation. You are unlikely to develop an empathic response if they are anxious about what might happen during the session or if they have unrealistic expectations. The more relaxed you can make them, the more you will pick up.

Ask them to keep notes so that they can analyse them afterwards. If they don't, you may forget an important piece of information as psychic impressions are as fleeting as dreams and easily forgotten when the moment has passed.

Initially you may need to ask them to tell you what areas of their life they would like you to explore. But this is just to help you attune, you are not asking for clues. The less information you are given, the better chance you have of getting a clear unbiased picture. When you begin to get impressions, trust them, even if they make no sense to you. Small or unusual details may have great significance for your client and constitute the validation you need.

Exercise 2: Tuning In

*One of the most effective methods of tuning in
is to raise your consciousness in single steps by
focusing on each of the chakras in turn and then
extending your awareness to your client's
corresponding chakra.*

◆ Once you are relaxed, focus your awareness
in the **Root chakra** at the base of the spine.
Visualize it saturated in red, the colour of
physical energy. As it opens you may feel a
prickly sensation or a subtle pressure similar
to that experienced when exploring the aura.

◆ Extend your awareness outwards to merge
with your client's aura and try to envisage
them going about their daily routine. You are
now tuned to the level expressed in the phrase
'I Have'. What impressions do you receive?

◆ Draw this energy up into the **Sacral chakra**,
beneath the navel. Don't simply imagine it.
Feel it as a subtle, almost physical force rising
through the centre of your body. As you do
so visualize the colour orange and extend
your awareness to attune to your client's
emotional well-being. You are now attuned
to the centre expressed in the phrase 'I Feel'.
Again, what impressions do you receive?

◆ Continue in this way rising in consciousness
through the other chakras as follows:
The Solar Plexus chakra This centre
encapsulates the sense of identity as
expressed by the phrase 'I Can'. Visualize
the colour yellow which corresponds to the
quality of energy associated with this centre

and visualize your client achieving their
ambitions. What are they?
The Heart chakra This chakra is green and
governs relationships. The corresponding
phrase is 'I Love'. Visualize your client with
their family and friends. What do you see?
What feelings overwhelm you?
The Throat chakra This chakra is blue,
symbolizing the quality of energy associated
with communication and self-expression. The
corresponding phrase is 'I Say'. Visualize your
client conversing with you. What would they
like to say? Is there something they are
struggling or reluctant to express?
The Brow chakra This centre is purple
symbolizing insight, intuition and ideas as
embodied in the phrase 'I See'. Visualize
standing beside your client looking out of a
window on the world. What do you see?
The Crown chakra This centre is white,
symbolic of the spiritual state expressed by
'I am'. Visualize your client surrounded by an
aura of radiant white light. Is there someone
from the other side with them? Is there a
darkness near them? If so, it could indicate
depression, illness or a negative influence.
Can you probe this and sense its origin?

At first this process should take about ten
minutes, but with practice you will be able to
stimulate each energy centre as readily as you
can recall the colours associated with them. You
may find it difficult at first to alter your centre of
consciousness from the head to another part of
your body, but refocusing awareness elsewhere
at will is essential for psychic work. And as with
all techniques it will become almost instinctive
with practice.

Communicating with spirits

It is a popular misconception that spirits are summoned at the request of the medium and because of this many people still believe that spirit communication is wrong because it disturbs the peace of the departed. In fact, the reverse is true. Spirits come only when they have something that they are desperate to impart to the living and they use a medium because most of us are not receptive to direct communication at their higher level of vibration. When they impress their thoughts upon us or affect appliances around the home we tend to dismiss it as a product of our imagination. But if we trusted these subtle impressions as evidence that they were watching over us we would strengthen the connection and develop a heightened sense of their presence.

Revealing Details

In his autobiography *One Last Time* the young American medium John Edward describes a typical reading that offered comfort and closure to one grieving family. In 1992 a bereaved mother and father came for a reading on the recommendation of a friend, although the mother was sceptical and distrusted mediums on principle. But as soon as they sat down John felt the presence of their daughter and described the circumstances of her death in detail. She had been killed in a car crash, but the police had concluded that no other vehicle had been involved. John revealed that she had, in fact, swerved to avoid another car that had crossed over into her lane forcing her to collide with a tree.

After the reading the couple hired a traffic accident investigator who re-examined their daughter's car and discovered traces of white paint on the bumper and other details which proved that John was correct. It also brought the parents some peace to know that it had not been their daughter's fault.

Psychometry

Psychic Detectives

In 1996 the UK *Psychic News* reported that Walter Smith, an American living in England, had recruited 12 local psychics to give a psychometric reading of a letter he had received from a contact in the FBI. The letter concerned the activities of the so-called Unabomber who had been terrorizing US institutions for 17 years with threatening letters and mail bombs. The psychics' impressions provided an uncannily accurate profile of the suspect arrested later that year prompting Smith's FBI contact to declare, 'I can honestly say they have made me a believer'.

Psychometry is the capacity to obtain intuitive impressions of a person by tuning into an object that they have handled. Metallic items such as watches and jewellery are ideal objects to work with as they readily absorb mental and emotional energy and retain the charge over a long period. But a highly sensitive psychic can 'read' impressions from a flower or a photograph if their client has handled it just before the session. It is one of the simplest and most easily acquired of all the psychic abilities. If you want to train yourself to do it, or if you want to find out if you already possess the ability, simply follow the test described in exercise 3, opposite.

The power of positive thought

The power of positive thought has been well-proven. It is the basis of innumerable self-help manuals and a cornerstone of modern psychotherapy. But the power of negative thought is just as real. And we need to be aware how easily negative mental energy can be transferred unconsciously from person to person.

A Book of Ghosts

A few years ago my wife and I were having trouble sleeping for no apparent reason. It was a quiet, pleasant evening and we were both exhausted after a long day looking after the children. Yet we still couldn't settle down. Something was disturbing us. After an hour or so I got out of bed with the intention of taking a walk round the garden, when I found myself drawn to something on the bedside table. I do not consider myself particularly sensitive to atmosphere, but it was emanating a disturbing presence throughout the room that was almost suffocating. It was a library book on the subject of ghosts, but it wasn't the subject nor the lurid-looking cover which was creating the disturbance in the atmosphere. I have read many books on a similar theme but I have never felt a presence such as that before or since, so it was not my aversion to the subject. It was the accumulation of mental energy that had been absorbed into its pages by successive readers brooding on the fearful stories. The moment I put it outside the oppressive atmosphere was gone.

The next time you are in a public library, choose a book at random and see what impressions come to mind just from handling it. But keep clear of the horror and true crime sections!

Exercise 3: Personal Impressions

Psychometry is a talent which intensifies with experience and one which has been called upon by archaeologists searching for artefacts and by the police who have used psychics to provide vital clues gleaned from the personal possessions of murder victims. You can test it for yourself using the following exercise.

◆ Ask a friend, work colleague or member of your family to obtain a personal item from someone that they know well so that they can later verify the impressions you receive. The item should only be handled by the owner, so get them to wrap it in a cloth or seal it in a box before passing it on.

◆ Then take the object in your palm and cover it with your other hand until you feel a warmth or a tingling sensation.

◆ Close your eyes and keep your mind blank. Accept whatever images come to mind. If a scene presents itself, enter the picture and allow it to lead you deeper into the environment.

◆ Describe aloud what you see so that your friend can make notes for subsequent analysis.

Mind to Mind

You can replicate Rhine's experiment with a friend to test your own ESP.

◆ All you need is five blank post-cards and a thick felt-tip pen.

◆ Draw one of the following five shapes on each card: star, cross, circle, square, three wavy lines. Hand them to your partner.

◆ While they concentrate on one of the images you relax into a meditative state so as to become receptive to their mental impressions.

◆ Let your mind go blank. Then trust the first impression that comes through.

◆ Initially, you may not receive an image immediately. If so, visualize your partner holding a blank card and alter your perspective so that you are looking over their shoulder. Which card are they holding?

Variation: Sit with your back to your partner and ask them to shuffle the cards then place them face up on a table in front of them. Using the same technique you can now reveal the order of the cards.

The most common argument against the existence of psychic phenomena is that it has yet to be proven scientifically. Fortunately the laws of the Universe do not require our verification before they can operate otherwise we would be living at the centre of the Universe on a flat Earth created in six days by a divine being and inhabited by sea monsters, dragons and giants. In the last 50 years science has been forced to recognize the existence of dark matter and the paradox of quantum physics. Biologist Rupert Sheldrake, author of *Seven Experiments That Could Change The World*, argues that it's only a matter of time before science identifies, quantifies and demonstrates the latent powers of the mind. It is his contention that we can extend our minds to tune into a collective consciousness in the same way that migrating animals do and that this ability may be an aspect of our survival instinct.

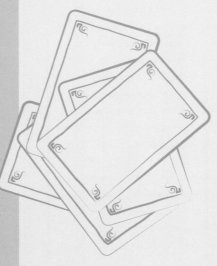

Rhine's Experiments with Telepathy

In the 1930s the father of experimental parapsychology, Dr J B Rhine, conducted an extensive series of tests over an eight-year period at Duke University in North Carolina, which made a convincing case for the existence of extrasensory perception (ESP). Using a pack of 'Zener', each with a simple image, he demonstrated that his subjects were able to guess correctly which card he was holding more often than could be attributed to chance. His most outstanding subject, a divinity student named Hubert E Pearce, beat odds of 22 billion to 1 by scoring 558 hits in 1,850 tests where 370 represented chance.

During the 1970s, ESP experiments were taken to a new level when researchers at the Maimonides Dream Laboratory in New York asked a subject to send images to a partner who was sleeping in the next room. The transmitter was told to concentrate on a randomly selected series of images – usually fine art prints – and when the receiver awoke they described their dreams in detail. Remarkably, 80 per cent of the time the receivers had dreamt of elements gleaned from the pictures.

nfluencing others

¯he ability of one person to influence the thoughts ⸱f another was demonstrated scientifically at the ⸱tanford Research Institute, California in 1972. In a ⸱ontrolled experiment a volunteer was wired up to a ⸱hotostimulator, an instrument that creates specific ⸱rain wave patterns. A second volunteer was isolated ⸱om the first in a specially constructed chamber with ⸱ouble layered steel walls to shield him from electro-⸱agnetic signals. The first subject was then asked ⸱ 'contact' the second in the isolation chamber by ⸱rojecting his thoughts through the steel wall. When ⸱e photostimulator was activated it created a specific ⸱attern of brain waves in the first subject which was ⸱eplicated in the second indicating that their minds had ⸱omehow tuned in to one another.

How to Become a Psychic Artist

What is psychic art?

Psychic or automatic art, as it is sometimes called, is not a modern phenomenon. The ancient Egyptians and the Greeks used it to communicate with the gods who personified an aspect of their own Higher Selves. But perhaps the finest example was Mozart, one of the most prolific and intuitive composers in the history of classical music. Although he was trained from the age of six by his father to play both the violin and piano, his ability to compose fully orchestrated scores with minimal corrections straight to manuscript, and without recourse to an instrument, suggests that his talent was intuitive rather than learned. More recently the Brazilian automatic artist Luiz Gasparetto has produced a series of paintings in the style of the great masters using only his fingers in a matter of a minute or less. More remarkable still is the fact that he can produce two pictures simultaneously without looking down at the canvas, one of which he draws upside down.

A clue to the phenomenon may be found in the true meaning of the word genius which derives from the Latin *'gignere'* meaning 'to give birth to' and originally referred to a person's guardian spirit or Higher Self – the source of their inspiration.

Exercise 5: Seeking Inspiration

◆ Set aside a specific time each day so that you impress upon the Unconscious that you are expecting a communication.

◆ Have a pencil in your hand and plenty of paper as it is important not to interrupt the flow when the inspiration comes. But don't be surprised if you switch over to write with the opposite hand and your writing or sketches differ remarkably from your usual style.

◆ Close your eyes and keep your mind a blank as you affirm to yourself that you are an open and clear channel for communication in whatever form it desires to take. Then be still and write or draw whatever comes to your mind, even if it is a crude doodle or nonsense. If nothing comes, write 'nothing'. The idea is to tease out whatever is bubbling under the surface in the Unconscious or, in rare cases, connect with a benign spirit which is seeking comfort.

◆ After a minute or so, repeat the affirmation and record whatever comes to mind.

◆ Repeat the process for 20 minutes or until something comes through. At first you will probably receive nothing or nonsense, but you will need to persist in flexing your psychic muscles just as you would if toning your body.

◆ When the breakthrough comes you will know it is a genuine communication as the flow of words or pictures will come faster than you can think of them and the quality will be beyond what you could consciously achieve in your ordinary waking state.

TASK: DRAWING

Using a sketch pad and pencil, plus watercolours, pastels or whatever medium you choose, place the pad on your lap and enter a relaxed meditative state. Ask your guides and Higher Self for inspiration then, on opening your eyes, begin by drawing a circle while holding your pencil very loosely so that it skims the surface of the paper. Start to shade the outline of the circle so that it looks like a tunnel then gradually extend the lines outward until it transforms into an eye. Draw the eye in detail, adding colour, and as you do so, sink deeper into relaxation and into the world which the eye symbolizes. Periodically close your eyes and while sustaining the image of the eye pass through it into the dimension beyond. Then open your eyes and draw what you see.

If at first you don't visualize anything complete the sketch of the eye then turn to a new sheet of paper and draw whatever comes to mind, allowing your hand to control the pencil, not your thoughts. Be prepared to cover every sheet with doodles and abstracts as you tease the visions to the surface.

Channelling inspiration

It could be argued that all creative people are psychic to a degree, in that they have learnt to apply their imagination productively to envisage what they want to realize in finite form. Even songwriters and 'serious' composers speak of hearing the music in their head before they shape it in sound. But what distinguishes a masterpiece from the mundane is the degree to which the artist is able to become a conscious channel for inspiration from the Unconscious or Higher Self. Psychic artists go one step beyond this level of consciousness, extending their awareness to draw spirit guides, ghosts and a host of celestial beings which inhabit the inner and upper worlds. When celebrated psychic artist Anne Brydges produced a painting of a friend's spirit guide it struck the friend as being a striking likeness of someone they knew who had died five years earlier. When questioned the spirit replied that it had come in a form that the friend would accept and trust.

Even those who acknowledge that they have no apparent talent can produce significant works of art when they have attained the light trance-like state. Antiques dealer John Tuckey produced a novel in the style of Charles Dickens at a speed faster than he could read it and in an ornate 19th-century copperplate script. And housewife Rosemary Brown claims to have channelled original compositions from Brahms, Beethoven and Liszt among others despite having minimal knowledge of music. Music scholars have acclaimed her work as remarkable, although orthodox science remains sceptical of the whole phenomenon. However, specialists in the mysteries of the human mind, such as the British psychologist Stan Gooch, are convinced such examples are genuine and claim that the source of such inspiration is the independent personalities in the artist's own psyche.

Soul Rescuing

Releasing unquiet spirits from their earthbound existence is the highest form of service to which a psychic can devote their talents. But soul rescuing, as it's known, can be an extremely testing experience and therefore should only be undertaken by highly experienced individuals, whose own physical and psychological health is sound. It is not enough to be a gifted psychic. To be successful in soul rescuing you should also be patient, compassionate, experienced with psychic healing and also be versed in counselling techniques. Dealing with an unquiet spirit is no different from dealing with a disturbed individual in the physical world. Both require you to be non-judgemental and exercise unconditional positive regard (empathic understanding).

Beginners should join an established group (local spiritualist churches, healing circles and meditation groups are a good contact point) and ensure that they have worked through the grounding and clearing exercises described elsewhere in this book before attempting to make contact.

Betty Shine

Celebrity medium Betty Shine has been dubbed 'the world's number one healer' by the press, but despite curing thousands of people around the world and introducing millions to psychic phenomena through her books and radio and TV appearances, she radiates the warmth and good humour you might expect of a favourite aunt: 'I haven't had any experience that has convinced me of the existence of evil, although I've had many frightening experiences with "negative entities" created by the human mind. On one occasion I saw a dark entity overshadow my patient and I heard it say, "I will never leave her, she is mine." As soon as I began praying for protection I saw a bright white light appear behind it, putting the figure into silhouette. It was clearly a man and as he was pulled away by some unseen force into the light he screamed. My patient covered her ears, though she later claimed that she hadn't actually heard the scream, but had acted instinctively. I later learnt that her first husband had been a possessive, sadistic man. After his death she remarried but she felt as if something was oppressing her. A few weeks after the exorcism the woman returned to my healing centre radiant and relieved, finally free of the black cloud she had felt had been smothering her for years. Such stories might deter those wishing to develop their own psychic abilities, but I received a valuable insight into the nature of "evil" from one of my guides. He told me that life in the spiritual dimension mirrors our own and so we should treat unpleasant entities the same way we would treat unwelcome visitors. Ignore them and turn your thoughts to higher and more pleasant matters. ... We are all psychic, but knowing that and acting on it helps to make you more receptive. You can't come to any harm by opening up for the simple reason that "Like attracts like". Most so-called psychic philosophy boils down to simple common sense.'

Exercise 6: Into the Light

◆ You may wish to clear the atmosphere, charge the room with positive energy and raise your consciousness in preparation for the work by playing suitable music lighting candles or burning incense

◆ Begin by casting a circle of white light around yourself and invoking your guides and the angels for assistance using the following words or words of your own choosing: 'In the name of Almighty God, creator of all living things, I ask for the presence, protection and assistance of my guides and Guardian Angels. May Raphael go before me, Gabriel behind me, Michael at my right hand and Uriel at my left while above me shines the six-rayed star, the living presence of God.'

◆ If you have been called in to 'clear' a property of a restless spirit the owner may have been able to tell you what you are dealing with otherwise you will have to probe the location psychically for clues or establish contact directly with the entity. It may be the spirit of a deceased relative or a previous inhabitant who is either unaware that they are dead, or who is unable to move on because they are confused or troubled by something that was unresolved at the time of their death. In any case, you should adopt a sympathetic tone, one that lets the spirit know that you are there to help. Only if it proves to be belligerent should you assert your higher will and command it to be gone. Knowing the name of a disembodied spirit will give you some degree of control over it as well as helping you to empathize with it as a troubled soul.

◆ Remember it is not enough that your intentions are good. You need to communicate with it in a language it understands. There is no point in using a Christian text for exorcism if the spirit was vehemently anti-religious in life, nor will New Age expressions prove helpful if the spirit was a devout church-goer. Use whatever words you sense it will respond to.

◆ When you have contact you may see an apparition, sense a presence or hear their voice. If the spirit is benign it should be sufficient to ask your guides to draw near and guide it to the light. However, if it is reluctant or resists you can call on its deceased relatives to invite it into the light from the other side. During the ritual you should continue to invoke the blessing and assistance of the Divine by calling on a spiritual figurehead such as Jesus or Buddha, reciting the Lord's Prayer (you don't have to be a Christian to do so), or repeating a sacred phrase. Use whatever you feel gives you strength.

◆ When you feel that the spirit has departed or you have seen it absorbed in to the light close down and clear the room by sprinkling salt at the four corners and at each entrance. Then thank your guides and the angels before you leave.

◆ Cleanse your aura by having a shower then go for a walk, preferably in a park or garden, to ground yourself and clear any residual energy.

◆ If you were successful you will have sensed the spirit's departure. If so, don't be surprised if it appears spontaneously during a subsequent meditation, radiant, healthy and as it was in the happiest time of its life.

A Guide to Symbols

Yin yang
In Chinese philosophy Yin symbolizes the dark, negative, intuitive and passive principle in the Universe and in ourselves while Yang is the light, positive, rational and active principle.

Eye and Third Eye
The source of psychic sight (clairvoyance) can be awoken through meditation and visualization, although many Western psychics stimulate it at will or find that it is activated spontaneously. Recent scientific research suggests that the source of these psychic visions is the light-sensitive pineal gland located in the centre of the forehead.

Sun
A symbol of the Universal life force and of vitality, creativity, rebirth and the male principle.

Moon
A symbol of the female principle and of the intuition and the Unconscious.

Stars
An ancient symbol of guidance, protection and constancy. The five-pointed pentagram or pentacle symbolizes harmony of the mind, the body and spirit but also the synthesis of the constituent elements of the Universe.

Horse and chariots

A traditional Hindu symbol of the Self later adopted by Jung to illustrate thought (the charioteer), willpower (the reins), the life force (the horses) and the body (the chariot). In traditional Kabbalah the process of raising one's awareness through meditation was known as 'rising in the chariot'.

Heart

An ancient symbol of truth, compassion and courage often equated with the soul or the sun.

Eagle

One of the earliest symbols of victory but also of aspiration, power, speed and perception.

Ladder (to another sphere)

Symbolic of the ascent to higher states of consciousness as in the Old Testament story of Jacob's Ladder.

Bridge

A universal metaphor for the passage between the physical and spirit worlds.

Mountain

The meeting point of the celestial and terrestrial realms and a symbol of stability, eternity and challenge.

Gate/door

A symbol of perception and opportunity.

Cross

One of the most ancient symbols. In the pre-Christian era it symbolized the four cardinal points of the compass, the four phases of the moon and the four elements, but also the containment of Universal energy. It also summarized the principles expressed in the Kabbalistic Tree of Life.

Pillar

Two pillars are frequently used in esoteric literature and ritual (such as in Freemasonary) to symbolize the complimentary principles governing the Universe.

Tree of Life

The central glyph of the Kabbalah, the philosophy at the heart of Jewish mysticism and the western esoteric tradition.

Hexagrams

Figures composed of broken and unbroken lines representing Yin and Yang in Chinese divination.

Mirror

In ancient times mirrors were used for scrying (clairvoyant visions) and considered as gateways to the invisible realms of spirit.

Crystals

Truth, purity. According to the writer Aldous Huxley crystals exert a fascination because they remind us of th structure of the inner worlds with their vibrant colours. They are commonly used for protection and healing.

Runes
A pictographic alphabet of Nordic origin often represented on stones used in divination.

Dolphin
Guide. In Greek, Cretan and Etruscan mythology dolphins embodied the qualities of speed, salvation, transformation and love – later they were adopted by early Christians to symbolize Christ.

Dove
Spirit. Since biblical times the dove has symbolized peace, purity, tenderness, hope and love.

Butterfly
Due to its life cycle the butterfly has been a symbol of transformation, regeneration and specifically the soul since ancient times.

Chakras
Chakra is the Hindu word for wheel and is the name given to the spinning wheel-like vortices of energy in the human body, although in Tibetan Buddhism they are commonly envisaged as blossoming lotus flowers.

Open book
To encourage the Unconscious to imprint its message on your mind try visualizing an open book during a visualization or picture one before you go to sleep.

Scroll
An iconographic symbol of wisdom and prophecy.

Diary and pen

It is important to keep a detailed record of your dreams and psychic experiences for analysis as they tend to fade from your memory with the passing of time. The only way you can verify a significant and possible precognitive vision is to have a dated record of the experience.

Art

The Higher Self is constantly seeking to communicate and will express itself in imagery rather than verbally, so indulge your creative urges to strengthen the connection with the Unconscious.

Hand

Healing. A general symbol of power, action, strength and protection. In palmistry the lines and mounts of our hands are considered highly significant.

Meditation

The practice of quietening the mind offers many benefits for mind, body and spirit as well as a means of heightening awareness of the greater reality beyond the material world.

Cosmic egg

An ancient symbol of the microcosm and the mystery of life and creation.

Angels

Angels have been envisaged as divine messengers but may also be projections of our own divine nature offering guidance, comfort and occasionally even physical protection in times of danger.

Ghosts

Ghosts are generally thought to be the residue of personal energy with no consciousness of their own and therefore harmless to the living.

Hourglass

A symbol of the passing of time and the transient nature of life derived from the combination of two triangles, one inverted to represent destruction and the other upright representing creativity.

Wheel

In Tibetan Buddhism the wheel is a symbol of the endless cycle of life, death and rebirth (see also Chakras) governed by the law of Karma (the Universal law of cause and effect).

Lotus

In traditional Eastern philosophy a blossoming lotus flower represents serenity and spiritual awakening.

Flame or torch

Symbolic of the life force, purification, enlightenment and the trial of the spirit through life.

Cards

There are many forms of cards used for psychic exploration, the most common being the traditional tarot cards, but contrary to popular belief none of them possess divinatory power of their own. They all serve as a focus for the reader's intuition and the degree of insight derived from the cards is entirely dependent upon the reader's insight.

Glossary

ANGELS Benign discarnate beings which may be a projection of our own Higher Self; Raphael, Gabriel, Michael and Uriel are angels referred to in the text. These four are derived from the semitic tradition and were assimilated into Jewish, Christian and Islamic mythology as the Semitic tribes dispersed in the second century BCE.

ANGEL MEDITATIONS A creative visualization exercise designed to raise awareness to the angelic (spiritual) level.

APPARITION A visual impression of personal energy in the ether.

ASTRAL REALM The next level above our physical/material world which we visit in our dreams. It is composed of etheric energy which can be manipulated by our mental energy (our thoughts).

ATOM Microscopic particle of energy.

AURA A field of energy surrounding the human body which can be seen and felt by those who have attuned to its higher vibrational frequency. It has seven layers, each one emanating from a specific chakra and coloured by the quality of energy in that chakra.

AURIC READING The practice of gaining mental impressions from tuning into someone's personal energy field.

BINAH The sphere representing Understanding and Reason on the Kabbalistic Tree of Life.

BLISS JUNKIE Someone who does so much meditation that, due to the natural high that results, they neglect their everyday responsibilities.

CHAKRAS See diagram on page 25.

CH'I The Chinese term for Universal energy or the life force.

CLAIRAUDIENCE The rare ability to hear the voice of spirit guides and those who no longer live in the physical dimension, for the purpose of giving guidance to other people. It is not to be confused with hearing the voice of your own inner guide or Higher Self.

CLAIRSENTIENCE The ability to sense the presence of discarnate beings such as ghosts, spirit guides and angels.

CLAIRVOYANCE The ability to see through physical barriers to other locations, and beyond to non-physical dimensions.

DAAT The non-manifest sphere on the Kabbalistic Tree, symbolizing the abyss we all have to cross to reach Enlightenment.

DÉJÀ VU A common phenomenon in which the person feels that they are re-enacting a scene from their life that they may have dreamt or acted out before, although they have no definite recall of doing so. Curiously, the event is usually of little consequence, often mundane and insignificant.

DISCARNATE BEINGS Spirit entities that are not at that moment in a human body.

DOPPELGANGER HALLUCINATIONS From the German word meaning 'double spirit', but the clinical definition of the phenomenon allows for a partial apparition of a ghostly transparency.

ESOTERIC The hidden or secret teachings underlying a religion as opposed to the orthodox form.

ETHERIC BODY A matrix of mental and emotional energy which takes on an individual's physical form at birth and resides in the body attached by an elasticated silver cord. Also known as the dream or astral body.

EXTRASENSORY PERCEPTION (ESP) The ability to perceive impressions and communications from the spirit world or from other human beings without direct physical or verbal contact.

FEDERAL BUREAU OF INVESTIGATION (FBI) The national law enforcement agency of the USA.

GEVURAH Sphere of Judgement on the Tree of Life.

GHOSTS A residual impression of personal energy left in the atmosphere. They can do humans no physical harm.

GREAT DREAMS Dreams of revelation and insight into the meaning and purpose of life.

GREATER REALITY The totality of existence beyond the physical world.

GUARDIAN ANGEL A personal protector and guide that is able to influence an individual from the spirit world. It is thought that it could also be a projection of an individual's own Higher Self which is triggered during a crisis.

GUIDES The living essence of an evolved soul who has chosen to return to Earth in order to help someone with whom they have an affinity.

HESED Sphere of Mercy on the Tree of Life.

HEXAGRAMS A group of six (broken or unbroken) lines used to form patterns in the I Ching.

HIGHER SELF The source of all our ideas, intuition and inspiration; the loving, compassionate, all-knowing source and centre of one's being.

HOD Sphere corresponding to the Intellect on the Tree of Life.

HOKHMAH Sphere of Wisdom on the Tree of Life.

JUNGIAN PSYCHOANALYSTS A branch of psychoanalysis subscribing to the theories of Swiss psychoanalyst Carl Jung.

KABBALAH The ancient Jewish metaphysical philosophy at the foundation of the Western esoteric tradition. It seeks to explain our place and purpose in existence through a symbolic diagram known as the Tree of Life on which are arranged the divine attributes which are manifest in finite form in every human being (see diagram on page 21). It envisages a pattern of interpenetrating worlds of increasing density namely the divine world of Emanation (pure consciousness), Creation (thought), the astral/dream world of Formation (spirit), and our own physical world of Action.

KETER The Crown of the Tree of Life symbolizing perfection and the Godhead.

KUNDALINI The powerful serpent energy of Hindu tradition which is said to reside at the base of the spine and be unleashed during the process of enlightenment.

LUCID DREAMS A dream in which the dreamer becomes conscious that they are dreaming and then takes control of the dream, manipulating the images at will.

MAJOR ARCANA The picture cards in the tarot pack.

MALKUT The lowest sphere on the Tree of Life symbolizing the material world and root of each of the higher worlds as the same glyph is repeated in the three higher worlds.

MEDITATION The act of quietening the mind.

MEDIUMSHIP The practice of attuning oneself to a higher frequency of awareness in order to receive messages from spirits.

MERIDIANS The network of vein-like lines carrying vital energy through the body.

METAPHYSICAL Pertaining to the non-physical realities.

MINOR ARCANA The number cards.

NATURAL LAWS Those laws which are the governing principles of the material world and proven scientifically to exist.

NEGATIVE ENERGY Personal energy disturbed by emotional or mental distress.

NEW AGE MOVEMENT A blanket term for various groups and individuals with a more holistic, spiritual and nature-centred world view.

NEZAH Sphere of Eternity on Tree of Life.

ORACLE A means of divining future events.

OUIJA BOARDS A dangerous tool for contacting spirits.

OUT-OF-BODY EXPERIENCE A common phenomenon in which the dream, etheric or astral body becomes temporarily detached from the physical while the individual is fully conscious of the separation.

PARANORMAL PHENOMENA Any incidents or experiences which defy a rational explanation.

PARAPSYCHOLOGY The study of mental phenomena such as telepathy.

PATHWORKING An advanced form of guided meditation which offers a symbolic map of the conscious and unconscious mind, known as the Tree of Life.

PHYSICAL LAWS The laws which govern life on Earth, for instance gravity.

POLTERGEIST A destructive spirit that some people believe could be suppressed mental energy, which might explain why they tend to appear in the presence of neurotic, intense or disturbed individuals and pubescent teenage girls.

PRANA Hindu term for the Universal life force.

PRECOGNITIVE DREAMS Dreams in which future events are perceived; also known as 'Prophetic dreams'.

PSI An abbreviation for 'psychic'; an informal term used by parapsychologists to describe paranormal phenomena.

PSYCHE The non-physical aspect of the human personality, for instance, thoughts and feelings.

PSYCHIC Derived from the Greek word *'psukhe'* meaning soul, and can be applied to either a person who claims to have developed a 'sixth sense', or an ability which appears to be outside the possbilities determined by 'natural laws'.

PSYCHIC ART Drawings or paintings created using one of the psychic senses, using impressions from the spirit world.

PSYCHIC HEALING The ability to heal the physical body by channelling the Universal life force to the source of the disease in the etheric body.

PSYCHOANALYSIS The treatment of mental problems and disorders through the study of the unconscious mind.

PSYCHOMETRY The capacity to derive impressions of people and places from objects.

READINGS The practice of gleaning impressions of a person's state of mind, health and even past lives by psychic means.

REM Rapid eye movement; the point in sleep where dreams occur.

REMOTE VIEWING The extension of awareness to another location.

RUNES Nordic symbols which can be used for divination.

SCRYING The art of foretelling future events by gazing into a reflective surface.

SENSITIVES Another word for practicing psychics; some will prefer this word, it signifying an acute sensitivity to the subtle energies surrounding all living things.

SIXTH SENSE The ability to perceive a greater reality beyond the physical dimension, usually involving clairvoyance.

SOLAR PLEXUS The pit of the stomach beneath the diaphragm.

SOUL RESCUING Releasing unquiet spirits from their Earthbound existence.

SPIRITS The essence of a deceased person; they may not be aware they are dead; they are troubled.

SUPER-CONSCIOUSNESS A heightened state of awareness beyond the physical norm.

SUPERNAL TRIAD The top three spheres on the Tree of Life.

SUPERNATURAL The greater reality that exists beyond the four dimensions of the physical world.

SYMBOLIC FORM A pictorial or abstract form which has significance or meaning.

TAROT (CARDS) A pack of 78 cards used for divination.

TELEKINESIS The ability to move objects by projecting mental energy.

TELEPATHY Non-verbal communication using psychic attuning of minds.

THEORY OF SYNCRONICITY The idea that apparently meaningful events occur purely by chance.

THIRD EYE The invisible organ of psychic sight located between the brows in the centre of the forehead.

THOUGHT FORM An apparition created by mental energy with no consciousness of its own.

TIFERET The sphere corresponding to the Higher Self on the Tree of Life.

TRANCE A state of mind in which the individual is detached from a perception of the material world.

TREE OF LIFE The central symbol of Kabbalistic philosophy.

TRUE NATURE Our Higher Self.

UNCONSCIOUS, HIGHER SELF OR INNER GUIDE Our divine spark or essence.

UNIVERSAL LAWS The governing principles of existence.

YESOD The sphere corresponding to the Ego on the Tree of Life.

YIN AND YANG According to Chinese esoteric tradition they are the two complimentary principles on which the manifest Universe depends. Yin is dark, negative, passive and female; Yang is light, positive, active and male.

Index

Acorah, Derek 95, 100
alpha brain activity 49
amputees, and 'phantom limbs'
   30
angel meditations 12, 81, 122
angels 77, 78–87, 120, 122
   angelic encounters 86–7
   and clairsentience 100
   and doppelgangers 79
   experiences of 80–3
   invoking for protection 85
   the library angel 79
   stories about 78, 80
anger, and mental energy 33
archetypes, and pathworking 20
art, psychic 110–12, 124
ASSAP (The Association for the
   Scientific Study of Anomalous
   Phenomena) 7
astral realm 122
aura 28–31, 32, 122
   auric readings 9, 25, 29, 31, 122
   cleansing 115
   colours and their significance
      30
   evidence of existence 30
   feeling the auric field 28
   and ghosts 92, 93
   seeing the first layer of the aura
      29
automatic art 110–12

Barrows, Gordon 78
Base chakra 26, 27, 31
beta brain activity 49
Betz, Hans-Dieter 37
Bohr, Niels 44
Brow chakra 27, 104
Brown, Rosemary 112
Brydges, Anne 112
Burnham, Sophy, A Book of
   Angels 83

Cayce, Edgar 42, 48
celebrity psychics 7
chakras 23, 24–7, 119
   and the aura 29, 31
   and balance 24
   centring 25, 26–7
   closing down 92
   memorizing 25
   tuning into 104
Churchill, Winston 14
clairaudience 25, 122
clairsentience 100, 122
clairvoyance 25, 99, 100, 122
collective consciousness 14, 108
collective unconscious 14–16, 57
Confucius 68
consciousness
   collective 14, 108
   expanding 15
   and mental energy 33
cosmic egg 120
cross, symbol of the 118
Crowley, Aleister 73
Crown chakra 25, 27, 104
crystal balls 65, 66
crystals 118

detectives, psychic 106
divination 39
doppelgangers 79, 122
dowsing 37, 39
dreams 40–63
   alpha and beta brain 49
   creating your own 46
   dream dictionary 58–63
   dream journal 50–1, 57
   emotional level 44, 51
   Great Dreams 43, 50, 123
   improving dream recall 45
   inducing a dream 43
   Jung and the house of psyche
      56–7

lucid dreams 43, 50, 52–4,
   123
   mental level 46, 51
   need for dream time 42–3
   people in 63
   physical level 44, 51
   precognitive 43, 47, 48, 49,
   spiritual level 46, 51

Edward, John 7, 95
   One Last Time 105
energy see mental energy
ESP (Extrasensory Perception)
   6, 7, 99–101, 123
   and experiences of angels 83
   and telepathy 108–9
etheric field 29, 123
exercises
   the angel's cloak 85
   the angelic counsellor 87
   astral visit 56
   casting the runes 69
   celestial security 84
   centring the chakras 26–7
   channelling healing energy 3
   the cloud 55
   consulting the oracle 68
   conversing with ghosts 93
   creating your own dreams 4
   dialogue with your dreams 4
   entering the light 17
   expanding consciousness 15
   exploring the path of the
      psyche 21
   feeling the auric field 28
   the Garden 19
   grounding 24, 102
   how to see a ghost 89
   improving dream recall 43,
      45
   inducing a dream 43
   the inner journey 20

into the light 114–15
kabbalah cards 71
keeping a dream journal 50
making contact with your
    guardian angel 82
psychometry and personal
    impressions 107
scrying 67
seeing the first layer of the aura
    29
seeking inspiration 111
tarot cards 73, 74
testing your own ESP 108
testing your PSI rating 97
treasure hunt 39
triggering a lucid dream 54
tuning in 104
extrasensory perception *see* ESP
    (Extrasensory Perception)

foreseeing the future 6, 65–75
    I Ching 66, 68
    kabbalah 70–1
    runes 65, 66, 69
    scrying 66–7
    tarot cards 65, 66, 72–5
Fry, Colin 95

Gainsford, Sylvia 47, 75
Garden exercise 19
Gasparetto, Luiz 110
Geller, Uri 7
ghosts 77, 88–93, 121, 123
    and clairsentience 100
    conversing with 93
    and energy 32
    and guides 88
    how to see a ghost 89
    sensing the presence of 92
    thought forms 90, 125
    see also spirits
Gooch, Stan 112
Greene, Graham 44
Grounding 24, 102
guardian angels *see* angels
guides 88, 123
healing 9, 25, 34–5, 124

using a pendulum for 38–9
Heart chakra 26–7, 104
Higher Self 13, 14, 16, 18, 100,
    123
    and guardian angels 83, 86
    and mediumship 102
    and psychic art 110, 112
Hopkins, Sir Anthony 79

I Ching 66, 68

Jung, Carl 14, 56–7, 68

Kabbalah 70–1, 118, 122, 123
Kekule, Friedrich von 44
Kilbraken, Lord 48
Kirlian photography 30

library angels 79
library books 107
lucid dreams 43, 50, 52–4, 123

meditation 14, 15, 120, 124
    angel meditations 12, 81, 122
    groups 102
    and visualization 18
mediumship 102–5, 124
mental energy 32–3
    channelling healing energy 35
    colours 32
    and dreams 57
    and ghosts 32, 92
    opening your mind to 32
    and pendulums 38
    and thought forms 90
meridians 24
Morehouse, Major David 98
Mount, Tamara 32
Mozart, Wolfgang Amadeus
    110
Myers, F W H 92

Nash, Jill 101
New Age movement 7

O'Brien, Richard 86
the occult 8–9, 11

out-of-body experiences (OBEs)
    6, 7, 52–3, 55

Page, Karin 91
pathworking 18, 20–1, 124
Pearce, Hubert E 109
pendulums 37–9
poltergeists 90, 124
positive thought, power of 106
precognitive dreams 43, 47, 48,
    49, 124
PSI rating, testing 10–11, 97
psychic, meaning of the word 6
psychic powers
    defining 6
    developing 8–9
    proof of 6
'Psychological Bulletin' (journal)
    6
psychometry 6, 9, 25, 106–7, 125
Puthoff, Dr H 96

remote viewing 6, 96–8, 99, 125
Rhine, Dr J B 109
Robinson, Chris ('the dream
    detective') 49
Root chakra 25, 26, 104
runes 65, 66, 69, 119, 125

Sacral chakra 26, 104
sacred spaces 36
    protection by angels 85
Schroter, Hans 37
Schwartz, Professor Gary 49
science 6, 108
scrying 66–7
Secret Self 22–39
    the aura 28–31, 32, 122
    the chakras 23, 24–7, 119
    extending your awareness 37–9
    mind energy 32–3
    physic healing 34–5
sensitives (practising psychics) 6
Sheldrake, Rupert 108
Shine, Betty 7, 114
sixth sense 6
Smith, Walter 106

Solar Plexus chakra 26, 104
soul rescuing 113–15, 125
spies, psychic 98
spirit guides 77–93
    and clairaudience 100
    sensing the guiding spirit 101
    see also angels
spirits 90, 92, 125
    and clairsentience 100
    communicating with 105
    messages from 91
    poltergeists 90, 124
    and soul rescuing 113–15, 125
    see also ghosts
SPR (Society for Psychical
    Research) 7
Stanford experiments
    on remote viewing 96, 97
    on telepathy 109
Stevenson, Robert Louis 44
surveys on psychic experiences 7
Swann, Ingo 7, 96
symbols 116–21
Szent-Gyorgyi, Albert 44

tarot cards 65, 66, 72–5, 125
    choosing your tarot pack 73
    key to the cards 74
    and pathworking 20

readings 75
seven-card spread 74
testing your PSI rating 97
three-card spread for guidance
    73
using with the Tree of Life 72
tasks
    analysing your dream diary
        57
    clearing 81
    drawing 112
    making an angel list 86
    making a sacred space 36
    memorizing the chakras 25
    reading a dream journal 51
    tuning into a vital message 99
    visualization 18
telepathy 6, 108–9, 125
Third Eye 18, 24, 65, 84, 89,
    116, 125
    and remote viewing 97
Third Eye chakra 25, 27
thought forms 90, 125
Throat chakra 25, 27, 104
Tibetan Buddhism 121
Tibetan lamas 90
Tree of Life 70, 118
    and pathworking 20–1
    and the Kabbalah 70–1

and the Tarot 72–3
True Self 23, 93
Tuckey, John 112

the Unconscious mind 9, 13,
    14–21
    accessing 18
    collective unconscious 14–16,
        57
    and dreams 42–3, 49
    entering the light 17
    messages from 83
    and psychic art 112
    and the subconscious 14
    tapping into 14–16
Universal Consciousness 14, 48
Universal energy 33
    and psychic healing 35

Van Praagh, James 7, 95
visualization 18
    pathworking 18, 20–1

West, Dame Rebecca 79
women, and psychic experience
    7

Yin and Yang 116, 125

Acknowledgements

Executive Editor Jane McIntosh
Project Editor Leanne Bryan
Executive Art Editor Leigh Jones
Designer 'ome Design
Production Assistant Nosheen Shan
Illustrator Line + Line